Why Not Do What You Love?

An invitation to calling and contribution
in a world hungry for your gifts

MARTHA JOHNSON

PEARL MEADOW PRESS

ISBN: 978-0-9843048-0-6
Copyright © 2010 by Martha Johnson, MEd.

Published by:
Pearl Meadow Press, 255 Pearl Street, South Hadley, MA 01075
Phone: 413-532-2579   Email: mjggdi@comcast.net

Graphic Design and Layout:
Persona
236 Pleasant Street, Amherst, MA
Email: doreen@newpersona.net

First Printing: January 2010
Manufactured in the United States of America

LIBRARY OF CONGRESS CONTROL NUMBER: 2010900018

WHAT PEOPLE SAY

"*Why Not Do What You Love?*, like a mirror you look at each morning, asks the simplest question in the world, and one of the wisest and most compassionate. It tells real-life stories about people who are neither famous nor rich, they just do what they love. The book both provokes and reassures, challenges and clarifies, and demands nothing from us readers except for one thing: that we care—passionately—about the life we have been given to live. And it's written by someone who has walked her talk."

—*EVE MARKO, Founding Teacher, Zen Peacemaker Order*

"Martha's voice is the one that tells you it's okay to be yourself. She offers the ideas and guidance you wish your parents and teachers had given when you were growing up. Opposite of a 'self help' book, it's a must-read bible for anyone who subscribes to the belief that there is a fulfilling life that is just meant for them."

—*ANGELA LUSSIER, Author of* The Anti-Resume Revolution

"Martha turns this issue of "calling" inside out and outside in. She persuades and entertains, educates and coaxes, with examples, meditations, and essays. Actually, anyone who is seeking greater fulfillment in their life will find this book an invaluable resource for their quest. As an executive coach, I found it chock full of powerful questions, quotes, and exercises that I cannot wait to use with my clients."

—*JILL DAVIS, Coach to Executives*

"If you have ever dreamed of being paid to do what you love, if you have ever yearned to use your talents to help make a better world, I urge you to read this book and follow its gentle guidance. It can deliver on its promise—to bring you to the place inside yourself where mysterious powers lay waiting to be discovered, powers that can help you create the life you have always dreamed of living."

—*TOM MONTE, Bestselling Writer, including* Unexpected Recoveries *and co-author of* Taking Woodstock.

"What a wonderful honor it is to be included in your book! I think you couldn't have picked a more important subject and it is so timely, as so many who had focused purely on making money now take stock of their lives and wonder how they find more meaning through helping others."

—*DAVID MAZOR, Founder of Reader-to-Reader*

MARTHA JOHNSON
IN PRINT OVER THE YEARS

"The Thought Selection Process: A Tool Worth Exploring," an article in the *Training & Development Journal of the American Society of Training and Development,* May 1982 (under the name of Martha Spice)

"For Radical Change, The Buck Stops Here," chapter included in *Leadership in a New Era, Visionary Approaches to the Biggest Crises of our Time,* edited by John Renesch, 1996 (under the name of Martha Spice, and with the collaboration of Alan Gilburg)

"Taking Personal Responsibility," an essay included in *Perspectives on Business and Global Change,* the Journal of the World Business Academy, March 1997 (under the name of Martha Spice)

Musing Along the Way: A Woman's Journey Looking at Her Life through the Lens of Chronic Illness, Book One, June 2002 (under the name of Martha Johnson Gilburg)
This book is still available. With an update and a new title, it is scheduled for republishing in 2011 by Pearl Meadow Press.

Why Not Do What You Love? An Invitation to Calling and Contribution in a World Hungry for Your Gifts, January 2010 (under my birth and forever-from-now-on-name, Martha Johnson)

DEDICATION

TO MY PARENTS, Richard and Betty Johnson, who gave me life.
I am deeply grateful.

~

TO MEDIUM JOÃO AND THE HEALING ENTITIES, who
freed my spirit to write about what really matters to me.

~

TO PRESIDENT BARACK OBAMA, who lifted my spirits when
he issued the call for us to take more responsibility for our
well-being as individuals, communities and as a nation.

~

TO ALL COMPANIONS ON THE PATH who yearn for ways to
express their truest and deepest selves during their lifetimes—and
those who have already found a way to do so.
You embolden my spirit.

~

TO ALICE, RACHEL, GAVIN, TEA, ETHAN, OWYNN, AND
ALL OTHER YOUNG PEOPLE OF A FUTURE GENERATION.
When you are ready to craft lives that work for you and
the world, I hope these words will still be available and still
relevant to your life quests.
You sweeten my spirit.

This book you have just picked up
has been a long time coming.
Perhaps I am living proof that it is never too late
to do what you feel compelled to do in life.

CONTENTS

AUTHOR'S FOREWORD

IT'S IMPORTANT TO ME THAT YOU KNOW at least part of why this book has come to be—and why now.

I tried to write this book twenty years ago. At that time, I was annoyed by what I saw as the limitations of the self-help literature that then filled bookstore shelves. Apparently, the solutions to every life problem could be solved in 3 tips, 5 steps, and 7 habits. I felt that those prescriptions were way too simple.

I believe that paying attention to what you love and actually having the courage to pursue it involves much more than a few steps. It's a process of exploration, giving permission; it's a labor of love and an act of courage. I also believe that when you are in your right niche and feeling fulfilled, other life issues seem to become more manageable. I wanted to write a book that told more of what I see as the deeper truth of the matter. In spite of my numerous initial attempts, I wasn't able to bring this dream to fruition—it was not my time.

So why am I writing this book now?

The fact that I'm in my 70th year has definitely caught my attention. I'm very aware of the uncertainty of my survival—a realization that seems to have eluded me in my youth. In case it has also eluded you, I'll state the undeniable truth: someday, you will no longer be on this earth, at least within the body you've inhabited for so many years.

The next question emerges gently and starkly. Since I am going to "die," how then will I live for as long as I am here? Where do I belong in the scheme of things? The question is not only for me, but for anyone at any age. How will YOU live? Where do YOU belong? How will YOU discover your right place?

And so, here we are. Feeling fortunate that I have loved my life and work over the years, I'm aware of a new challenge as I age. In my remaining days, I want to recraft doing what matters to me in a way that accommodates my lower level of stamina, decreased mobility, and emerging gifts as a wise elder. I resonate deeply with the question, "Why not do what you love?," and even the exhortation, "Why NOT do what you love!" Both bring me full circle to observing from a fresh perspective what has always fascinated me: people employing their natural talents in the world to their own and everyone else's benefit.

I want to admit to you that I have no formal credentials in social research, nor do the thoughts and conclusions contained herein depend on any process of in-depth, statistically significant interviews. I am simply a very appreciative observer of those who seem to be doing what they love, and doing good in the world at the same time. It is a joyful lens through which to look at the world—a world which seems to need our talents—right now.

Apparently this is my particular Calling, or at least one of the ways it is being expressed right now. I have always loved asking thought-provoking questions. I was obsessive about asking them to myself and tried to take the next steps in my life in response to whatever answers I was willing to give myself at the time. My journey was—well—my journey, doing what I really loved and was challenged by. I have few regrets about my life.

Now retired from business, I have loved compiling these current observations and conclusions about others who have found their path in life. I write to promote the possibilities for the deep level of meaning and fulfillment that I believe can exist for all of us, both personally and professionally. I have organized this book around a question: Why not do what you love? This is an important question for all of us. Why? Because...

First, it's personal!

Doing what you love is less stressful and more healthy than just working to put food on the table—which, I admit, sometimes becomes a temporary necessity. I was saddened but not surprised to have met a woman recently who, upon learning I was writing this book, stated: "I don't like what I do anymore. Particularly in this economy. And I've been sick a lot recently. Do you think there is a connection?" Frankly, yes, I do. I met another woman who, in the face of the same difficult economic conditions, had decided to piece together her livelihood based on her interests and talents. She cleaned houses, she cleaned cars, she mowed lawns and cleaned yards. She painted seasonal pictures on the windows of small stores. You know what? She was so happy! She was doing the things that gave her intense pleasure, and she had time to be at home when her kids needed her. When you are doing what you love, living your authentic Self, furthering your life purpose, you never get bored. In business, you have no competitors when you are expressing your unique and special gifts. In your neighborhood, keeping up with the Jones' is no longer an issue. You are automatically more fun to be with when you are enjoying yourself both at work and at play. You are a great model for your kids and for others around you.

For those whose gifts fall into long-range visionary thinking, it's deeply and personally gratifying to help craft the new systems and new models that work for both the people and the planet. Particularly at this time and place. The natural gifts of pioneering personalities are definitely welcome because...

Second, it's planetary!

Imagine how lightly one could live on the planet when one is healthy and happy and aware of really only "needing" what money can't buy. Imagine how a commitment to health and happiness can ripple out to address the health of our families and the isolation in our communities! The goals of "more" and "better" which pretended to serve us for the last 70 years are under scrutiny.

It appears that having "more" and leading a "better" life can no longer easily co-exist if we hope for a sustainable future. We can now see how producing and consuming "more" led to a diminished quality of life across the globe. What happens when we eat the overly processed, genetically altered, and sugarified food? How and where do we dispose of our daily waste and our no longer new "stuff"? What is the impact of our high energy usage on the climate patterns, and how does it shape the lives we hope for our grand-children? How will we assure clean and sufficient water worldwide? Some people have more, but for most, it's definitely not "better." And it's starting to affect all our lives.

The desire for less stress, more community, clean air and water, peace, a meaningful life—the things we consider "better"—no longer has much to do with "more." This emerging awareness will hopefully invite us to reframe our existence as a quest for "enough." Enough in a way that also insures and allows enough of what's important for future generations, as well.

In this book, I present my own three powerful questions to support, and perhaps even accelerate, the process of self-initiated change. I do so with the humble recognition that the greater truths about strategies for living well are too big for any one person, or any one book, or any number of guidelines, to get their arms around. All books and guides to life are incomplete, including this one. Please consider the musings contained herein as my way of seeing and saying something that seems important to share. Use this book for whatever assistance it offers you, and keep looking for the tools and processes that will satisfy your needs and your learning style.

Most importantly, I believe that "when the student is ready, the teacher will appear". To state it another way, when one holds deep intentions for change, for fulfillment, for service, the path forward will emerge. The best we authors can do is to share what we see. I write to make my observations available to others who are ready to grapple with a particular piece of life's puzzle at this particular point in time.

That said, I am pleased to notice how many people don't need this book. They are those who are already in their right livelihood. We can find them merely by reading the paper, watching TV, and looking around town. They are those whose presence sustains and uplifts our spirits, while they solve problems both practical and planetary.

For instance, my neighbor Rocky doesn't need this book and never did. He's retired from a very satisfying career as a highly effective operations manager of a local manufacturing plant. Although he never graduated from high school, his natural intelligence, as well as an extreme curiosity to learn what it took to do each job better and to save the company money, kept him learning and growing. He had a talent for investing his resources and thus has retired comfortably. He now generously does the annual tax returns for each member of his extended family. Rocky retired on his own terms; walks the neighborhood daily; is a magnificent mentor to his 3 grandchildren; collects advice and information from every source under the sun; and dispenses it freely to all who ask. When we meet, I always ask him how he is doing. Day after day, year after year, he's been giving me the same answer, "I'm always doing great!" He's an incredible source of good cheer, good help, friendship, and a model for me in many ways.

Nor does my chiropractor need this book. He has already been "called" to the profession of hands-on healing. How do I know this? Beyond the training, knowledge and experience he has, his presence alone is a healing experience. The way he talks to his patients, cares for them and follows up with them—with joy and compassion—is a wonderful gift. It is easy to see that he considers his patients a gift to him, as well. His practice is full, and he is able to be present to each patient, even on the busiest days.

People using their innate gifts in professions they love seem to be the naturals. They are those who spend their lives gathering experiences through a career or a major avocation that brings an integrity to their lives. They live their purpose and their destiny and often acknowledge it using the very same words: "This is what I was meant to do."

Should we choose to face into the uncertainty of our survival, with a fullness of presence, we might discover that it galvanizes our most passionate, creative responses ushering in a renewed capacity to live in balance with all of life.

— CHRIS LANDRY, THEGREATTURNINGFILM.ORG —

I sincerely believe that each one of you can step into the same flow and join them, by acknowledging your own best gifts and by choosing to share them for yourselves and with others. When you invest in yourself and answer the call from within, something useful ripples out. Enough ripples can ultimately influence the social infrastructure we all depend upon for health, justice and community well-being. Why not do what you love? The question is clearly both personal and planetary, because in finding your own answers, you will change the world.

Yes, I also wrote this book in part because I am concerned about the challenges of the times in which we live, and I want to make a Contribution to people who face these challenges. As I talk to friends, read the papers, and see the newscasts, I find that people everywhere are trying to stay afloat. They seem to be focused on the search for a "job," or on trying to remain "employed". Their focus may be: "How will I support myself?" or "Who's going to want what I know how to do?"

While those are legitimate questions, they may be limiting. I invite you to deliberately consider broader and deeper queries like: "What do I love?" and "How do I want to serve?" I believe that if you focus on discovering your best gifts, and explore ways to use these gifts, your search for stability will contain more durable hope and less fear. In my view, there will always be a "job" for those so exquisitely centered in life that their Calling is also their Contribution.

Given all of this, I return to where I started. I'm going to die some day. At 70, I am well beyond the middle years. In the meantime, the question is still real for me. What do I love? And how will I use my remaining days?

One answer is this book.

Martha Johnson
November, 2009

INTRODUCTION

*"When we live in the close-knit ecosystem called community,
everyone follows and everyone leads."*
—*Parker Palmer*

TODAY, OCTOBER 16, 2009, I was surfing television channels. I caught a portion of a Steven Moore interview (senior economics writer for the Wall Street Journal) on the CSPAN call-in show, the Washington Journal. He was being asked a question by a student on behalf of herself and her peers: "When I graduate from college, where will the jobs be for me?" His answer— one he's given many times to college audiences across the country—was: "Do what you love!" Obviously I agree. What better time than now to do what will always make you a better job competitor, and allow you to feel fulfilled in the process? His advice to that student has been a passionate pursuit of my own for lo these past 40 years. And I was glad to see the advice that has always made sense to me, now coming almost daily from mainstream mouths.

My hope is that readers of all ages, in whatever stage of their life journeys, will find this book enriching to their quests for fulfillment. I've already noticed that **ELDERS** enjoy a prompt to reflect on their lives of calling and contribution in terms of choices made well or poorly, or in terms of delights and disappointments from which they have learned. Those elders who are wanting to look back to gain life perspective may be willing to share their wisdom with younger members of their families. Revisiting calling and contribution puzzle pieces and how they fell together, the dots connecting or not, the meaningful whole created or not, make a wonderful family legacy.

I've noticed that **BOOMERS** who thrived in boom years are starting to leave the workforce, seeking to make what's left of their productive years pay off in more ways than one. When I went to the doctor's office recently, I had in hand Mary Catherine Bateson's *Composing a Life*. The middle-aged nurse took a look and said, "Wow, just what I need! When I was 25, I thought I had planned out my life and that by the time I got to 50, I wouldn't have to worry. NOT! We have to keep reinventing."

I've noticed that today's **RECENT GRADUATES** are struggling to enter a very changed job market, and may be forced sooner than later to choose for themselves, rather than for the money, the prestige or the status. They may be looking for a new approach to employment seeking. And they may be looking to be useful in addressing community and world needs. One astute graduate of an elite college, whose Wall Street job offer was withdrawn due to the failing economy, sounded ready for something different when he said: "It was probably a gift in disguise. I wasn't much into banking anyway. I'll have to re-look at my situation."

I've noticed that many are **WANTING TO REASSESS** their options, redirect their efforts, or reevaluate their lives. At whatever age and for whatever reason, they are asking an important question: *Given the challenges facing the world, and my desire to leave a better place to the next generation, how can I use my time and my talents in ways of which I can be proud?*

What I hope every reader (and I include the coaches, counselors and helpers who may be sought out to provide guidance in this process) will find in these pages are many thought-provoking ideas for your consideration. You will find conversation starters, prompts for reflection, an impetus to share your life story with others. You will also find plenty of encouragement to get into action so that you can create your own islands of meaning, joy and service in our currently challenging world.

Part One opens the conversation about "calling" and "contribution" with very broad strokes, using the examples of others. When you discover and act on your own, most true impulses, where can it lead? What are the possibilities that resonate for you as you consider the variety of ways and venues to which others have been called?

Part Two begins laying out the queries you may want to ask yourself. You get a chance to explore what you know about your unique passions, gifts, desires and calls to service—the ones you may already be expressing, and the ones you may want to express more consciously.

Part Three invites you to pause. You will have arrived at a place where you may have gotten some of the information you need about yourself. How might you want to proceed?

Part Four provides a "big nudge" for you to tell more of the truth about what you really want to be or do—no matter how new or intimidating.

You get the opportunity to align your intentions at all levels, and to admit and transform any reluctance you are feeling about going for what you feel compelled and excited to do.

Part Five offers guidance illustrated by those who have taken action on their own behalf in the world. Hopefully it will serve as inspiration for some of the ways you may choose to move forward onto your desired life path.

Part Six acknowledges that as life proceeds, natural talents form into new and uniquely clustered gifts. Life purpose may take different forms, and it's important to return to reflection: "What's my authentic role at this time in my life on the planet?"

An **Appendix** contains a few resources that I have found useful to the life-shaping process which are beyond the scope of the book to discuss in detail.

And finally, I offer this gift in hopes that you, the reader, will find your right place, honor the beauty of your own gifts, and dare to express them. Allow the questions and the examples of others to lead you "home" to yourself. Know that you may find some sections easier than others, depending on your own comfort with reflection and introspection. Have patience with your inquiry and be willing for it to last as long as it takes.

It's important to remember that the questions, the steps, and the illustrations contained herein are not designed to "prescribe" answers for your life. Rather, they invite reflection, point a direction, and offer some gentle guidance. After all, it is only your own best answers that will work for you. Your best answers will come when you seek them, when you are ready for them and when you have the courage to lean into them.

The world awaits you—and me—no matter how old we are!

PART ONE

Take Time to Ponder
Your Possibilities

TAKE TIME TO PONDER YOUR POSSIBILITIES

I HOPE YOU ARE CURIOUS ABOUT YOUR LIFE and what it can teach you. I hope you are the kind of person that enjoys reflecting and looking within for your own wisdom. I hope you are one of those ready to say "yes" to a fulfilling and satisfying life that matters in the world. I hope you are one of those who have come to a place in your life where you find the following questions interesting, provocative, fun, and even necessary.

- A younger reader may be considering, "How can I craft a life that makes a difference?" wondering how you might have more influence over bringing your dreams to life.

- A reader in mid-career may have been attracted by the title tag line about the world being hungry for your gifts, and may be wondering, "What part of my own personal hunger might be assuaged by giving more of what I have to give?"

> Curiosity is, in great and generous minds, the first passion and the last.
>
> — SAMUEL JOHNSON

- A reader nearing retirement years may be asking, "Did my life have any meaning?" wondering whether their time on earth mattered and if there is still time left to make it meaningful.

In Part One, you'll have a chance to check in with yourself and explore the terrain of calling and contribution with a wide lens. You'll have a chance to consider the notion of "calling" and begin to contemplate how it might relate to your own life—your talents and passions and skill sets. Through the many examples from the lives of others, you'll have a chance to see calling and contribution in action.

Remember, this is a time to relax and ponder possibilities for yourself through the stories of others. Not only is it important to note the variety of

> As we find our way into our authentic self, the community of life will blossom forth.
>
> — BRIAN SWIMME, COSMOLOGIST, YOUTUBE VIDEO —

skills and talents on display in the following chapters, it is intriguing to note on what stage individuals are "called" to play their game. Some play their game with their family and friends, making a decided difference mostly visible in a very local setting, such as a school or community.

I also highlight people whose gifts call them to a larger arena, that of business, managing large organizations, and even changing the way the world works. As I will say in other places, callings do differ in scope of impact, but there is no difference in importance. **What's important is that you do what is yours to do on this planet at this time.** I hope you'll be genuinely amazed and excited by the stories, and I invite you to ponder options and possibilities for yourself as you begin to consider where and how you want to play your life game with the time that remains to you.

At the end of each chapter you will find a box containing either questions for deeper REFLECTION or further RESOURCES for your enjoyment.

Since the answers that will best work for your life are always and only your own, I encourage you to set aside some time and space to sit with each chapter as you read it and see what ideas and insights emerge for you.

CHAPTER 1

❧

You Do Have a Calling

"A musician must make music, an artist must paint, a poet must
write if he is to be ultimately at peace with himself.
What one can be, one must be."
—*Abraham Maslow*

I HAVE LONG BEEN AN OBSERVER and an admirer of people who seem
to be operating out of a sense of joy and purpose—people who love what
they do and who have organized their lives around what is important to
them. It has been my life goal to do the same. As a life and work coach, I
hold the possibility that my clients can do this as well.

You can recognize these people pursuing their calling everywhere: in the
hair salon, at the bank, on the subway, at work, in a newscast, somewhere in
your community. One signal that you are in their presence is how good you
feel. These people are doing what they love to do; they are doing it easily,
naturally and well, and just exuding pleasure and passion in the doing of it.
Challenges for them are merely bumps in the road that produce the thrill in
having something to overcome or sweep out of the way. People who follow
their calling seem to approach their chosen field with the artistry, flair and
uniqueness of their personal gifts. They seem to be at peace with themselves,
perhaps because the puzzle pieces for a life of meaning have been found, and
have fallen together. Their work seems easy, effortless and enjoyable.

Very simply, "calling" implies being called. In the past, it has been primarily applied to those in religious professions, those who "heard" a "call" from
God to join the priesthood, the ministry or the monastery. I believe it
deserves a broader application. Many people feel the "pull" to do something
specific in their lives. From whom the call comes might depend on one's
philosophy of life. But there is a "pull" from inside—recognized or

unrecognized, accepted or denied—that compels one to follow a path even, perhaps, without question.

It just feels right. It has to do with how you feel about what you are doing or wanting to do in life. Many people are already "following their call" because they can't help it, and they just may not notice it. It is characterized by the fact that you tend to do that particular thing—whatever it is-anywhere, anytime, no matter the money. You have found a good horse, the saddle is comfortable, and you are ready for a ride that will continue as long as it feels right.

There are other words I will use interchangeably with calling. Those who are exercising their calling could be seen as *expressing their essential selves, doing what they were born to do, living their destiny,* following their *soul purpose,* playing in *their niche,* pursuing a *vocation, living their right livelihood,* doing what is *a right fit for their gifts,* or playing their *authentic role.* While many people may find themselves doing many things they love to do throughout their lives, those who are expressing their calling seem to all say a version of the same thing: "This is what I was meant to do, and this is where I was meant to be."

I'm sure books exist on the nuances of difference among each of the phrases that for me signify *following one's calling.* For instance, the common term "right livelihood" is from the ancient Buddhist tradition. It is the fifth spoke of the eightfold path, which includes right speech, right action, and right intention. Social entrepreneur Bernard Glassman states in his book *Instructions to the Cook: A Zen master's Lessons in Living a Life that Matters* that right livelihood, according to the Buddha, is "doing what sustains all of our life, our spirit, our learning and our social action, in a way that does not harm any part of it." The way I translate this for myself is that what I love deeply nourishes me as it nourishes all around me.

While I want to acknowledge that each term has its unique source and nuance and can be described in much more depth, I am happy to leave that task to others. For me, each phrase mentioned above resonates as a way to talk about what each of us is born to do, whether or not we are actually doing it right now. When I use one of these phrases, feel free to substitute whichever phrase most speaks to you.

It has become clear to me that finding one's calling is not the result of making a career plan. Nor is one's calling necessarily a job title, such as teacher, mechanic or doctor. Rather, it seems to be is a unique combination of talents, passions, and skill sets, which may or may not fall into phrases most typically found in career development guides. Instead, there are special and individual *gifts* which allow teachers, mechanics, or doctors to be "very unique" in how they perform their craft. Consider how easy it is for us to see the difference between a teacher or a mechanic who is "putting in their hours," and those who are expressing some essence of themselves and who experience some thrill about the purpose of work that goes beyond "the job." Personally, I want to be served by those who are fully engaged in providing a service to which they are personally drawn.

If calling is not a job description or a title, what is it? What are these qualities that seem to resonate deeply in a person's being? Very simply, they are absolutely anything. Weird or wonderful, they are what you love, what you do well, what makes you smile, what makes your heart sing. With training or without, your gifts are the things you do better than most. They are the natural talents with which you were born. They are your passion, something you cannot not-express (double negative intended). In their expression, they also prove to serve others-no small part of what also brings joy and affirmation to one's own life.

To give you an indication how life calling can express itself beyond any particular job title, I'll recount a conversation I had with a woman named Sharon. I have reached the age where I can no longer touch my toes or manipulate a clipper, so I began going to the local senior center to have my toenails tended. Sharon is a delightful nurse who visits Mondays twice a month to provide this and other services. On my third visit—as I often do when I find someone who seems to love what they do—I launched into one of my "calling conversations".

"You seem to really enjoy your work," I broached. "What is it you like best about it?" She responded, "I love clipping and trimming, and straightening and taking the dry skin away."

"Would you say that is your calling?" I asked more directly. She giggled. "It feels funny to say that clipping toe nails might be my calling. I would consider my first calling is to be a nurse."

She paused and a smile crept into her eyes. "Actually, clipping and trimming is also what I love about gardening. I love to mow, rake, and take the dead leaves away. And I love trimming my daughter's hair." I could see the wheels turning as she reflected on the core similarity of everything she loved to do in her life.

She continued: "You know, I've pieced together my life, now, as a working wife and parent. I get to work part-time, clipping and tending, doing a part of nursing that I really enjoy—in different places, with different people, earning a good living. I also have time to be the Mom I want to be for my two kids in the afternoons, evenings and weekends; and I cut my family's hair and trim the dog. AND ALSO, I get to save us money at home by landscaping, gardening, mowing, and raking and removing the garden waste. Overall, I do think my life works for me right now."

Our conversation meandered and my toes were tended. I thought to myself, "She's an ordinary person who has really pieced together a good life, doing what gives her pleasure and extending that attention to her clients and her children." I noticed her smiling more broadly when I left and she thanked me for the conversation. Maybe she was celebrating on the inside. She now knows she's living her truth, her calling and her knowing. My guess is that she had never before consciously acknowledged the serendipitous wisdom of her own choices.

When asked about "calling," folks like Sharon may be a little intimidated by the concept, thinking it means you have to be SOMEBODY doing SOMETHING very SPECIAL. My conversation with her seemed to catalyze her recognition that, despite just being an "ordinary" wife and mother, she'd made her life work pretty well doing so many things she loved. She had managed to create both a life that works and a life that counts.

Sadly, some people have lost touch with their gifts and haven't built their lives around them—consciously or unconsciously. If they happened to have been a naturally gifted artist or musician born to lawyers or scientists, they might have been underappreciated in general, or told they should be more analytical. As children, they may have believed the advice from those in authority who squelched their unwelcome preferences. Or, there may have been another family dynamic in which a person's essential self was squashed by siblings, parents or other relatives.

If one's "essential self" is not welcomed within the family, it is much safer to hide. The deeper problem with this strategy is that in hiding from one's family, one often hides from oneself. Consciously or unconsciously, one may lose touch with those hidden aspects. Hopefully the questions in this book will help you illuminate for yourself any parts that were not named or noticed, or given value. These same parts may be the most unique and the most needed today, by you and those around you.

Whatever the reasons for losing touch with one's self, it is never too late to capture what is true. In a world hungry for your gifts, you, too, may be hungry—to express your own gifts. Perhaps I'll say that one again. **In a world hungry for your gifts, you may be the one who is starving.** You deserve to be a poet, a philanthropist, a musician; to comfort pets, build a socially responsible business, sing opera, ski or travel or change the world. You deserve to write, listen, organize, envision possible futures, make sense of things, fix stuff, tackle the world's problems—to do whatever you love to do best. All those activities can be done full time for pay. Or, if you have not found a way for your passion to support your lifestyle, you can become more aware of how sharing your natural gifts can claim more of your day voluntarily—for your own fulfillment and in service to your neighbors.

There is no failure in this game. It is not an all-or-nothing proposition. You can find an hour a day, or regular vacations, to do exactly what you love. You can support the causes and go to the meetings of people who share your passions. And, contrary to what many have learned to believe, it is possible to get paid for just about anything. The TV host of "Dirty Jobs" gets paid to do what he loves, messing around in the dirtiest jobs that exist and highlighting some of the really tough professions that make this country work. A recent acquaintance lit up when she talked about her part-time job doing autopsies, being a detective and searching out clues as to cause of death. She's "dying" to make it a full time gig. (Pun intended.) Start big or start small, but start uncovering your own desires. Start naming and filling your own needs. If you wait until you are sure that you will not make a mistake, you will spend your life waiting. Adopt one of the major tenets of this book: **When you do what is really right for you, you will generally be doing something that also is right for others**, and that leads us to consider how inextricably entwined are calling and contribution.

Reflection

Forget the question "What is my calling?" For now, just start with...

- What do I love?

- What do I do easily, wherever I am?

- What parts of my life do I really enjoy?

CHAPTER 2

❧

Your Calling Matters

"It's the little things citizens do.
That's what will make the difference.
My little thing is planting trees."
—*Wangari Maathai*

AS I'VE BEEN RAISING THE ISSUE OF "CALLING" with friends and colleagues and even strangers, it's always been a mutually provocative and entertaining conversation. Suddenly I began to notice how often the notion of contribution surfaced in these discussions. The joy of doing what one loves seemed always to be enriched by serving others. and by making a difference outside of oneself.

For instance, during my 50th high school reunion and the subsequent renewed connections with friends from the past, I noticed a pattern. Increasingly articulated was the desire to "matter," to help out, to do something that makes a difference in our confusing, problematic, depersonalized, and troubled society. Because these conversations occurred in the opening days of 2009 and the new Obama administration, they were often peppered with, "And our president is asking us to serve. I'm trying to figure out what I can do."

The connection between calling and contribution was brought into stark relief quite serendipitously. I was in the gym, on the bicycle, in front of a TV tuned to the ESPN channel—which I would never otherwise be watching. The show profiled retired Navy Captain Ed Nicholson, who, upon leaving the military, had had high hopes of spending his leisure days as an outdoorsman, his deepest love. But there was a nagging issue for him: "What about the men at Walter Reed who have been so injured in body and mind that they have lost much of the pleasures they had hoped to return to? Wasn't there something I could do for at least a few of them?"

Thus was born Project Healing Waters-Fly Fishing in 2005, now operating in 50 locations across the nation. **Visit www.projecthealingwaters.org.**

Captain Nicholson, and the numerous individuals and organizations he recruits, train veterans in fly casting on the grounds of Walter Reed and other VA hospitals. These volunteers teach skills that build limb strength and confidence. Then they take the vets, free of any charge, to the best river spots around the country to enjoy fly fishing, good companionship, and the healing powers of the natural world of waters and woods.

This television report about Captain Nicholson aired during the same week that I'd had "calling" conversations with my friends. I realized that I needed to expand my thinking. My original purpose was to write about "calling." Now it was expanding to include the dimensions of contribution. In that moment I was struck with the inseparability of "calling" and "contribution."

Captain Nicholson is still being an outdoorsman in his retirement, and he is applying his natural gifts and passions to a larger purpose. He has enlisted the time, talent, and energy of the like-minded to do the same. The testimonies of personal growth and change that have occurred on these river trips are profound and powerful. Combat veterans' souls are being soothed and their lives are returning to them in so many ways. The Captain and his friends discovered that the "we," the connection, the community, and the more-than-me is a substantial and enduring contribution to solving our societal ills. In the person of Captain Nicholson and his outdoor-loving friends, calling and contribution are two sides of the same coin.

While calling and contribution are different in concept, I notice it is hard to separate them in practice. In every example given in this book, people doing what they love to do and do naturally are really making a difference in someone else's life as well. We give up nothing when we serve with our passions. A special benefit accrues when we know that our natural gifts are bringing joy and help to those in need. Service enriches the server. Giving and receiving are one. All the platitudes apply. **It seems a fairly simple concept that by paying attention to the intersection of our natural gifts, our deeply held values, and at least one of the many needs around us, we connect to what we were born to do.**

Contributions can be the "small" things that really make a difference—

a Blockbuster employee that delights in always finding just the right movie for each patron, or the health club employee at the service desk who greets everyone with his animal towel origami. Contributions can be the "large" things, too. For example, as a 24-year-old graduate student of Yiddish literature, Aaron Lansky founded the National Yiddish Book Center on the grounds of Hampshire College in 1980. **Visit www.yiddishbookcenter.org.**

Realizing that irreplaceable Yiddish books, the legacy of 1000 years of Jewish life in Eastern Europe, were being discarded by American-born Jews unable to read the language of their parents and grandparents, he organized a national campaign to save them. Lansky tells his riveting story in his book, *Outwitting History: The Amazing Adventures of a Man Who Rescued a Million Yiddish Books*, 2005. His mission continues. A new wing of the Center opened in 2009 and will house a national school for Jewish culture. While there is a difference of scope between what I have referenced as "small" things and Aaron Lansky's "large" thing, there is no difference in the value of the giving, because each provider is simply doing some of what they came to earth to do.

And yes, little things can grow into large things. Wangari Maathai started planting trees to address the problems of deforestation, soil erosion, and lack of water in Africa. For that "little thing," she received the 2004 Nobel Peace Prize.

Reflection

Where in your own life can you see the calling and contribution connection?

How do you feel about what you see— or don't see?

Think of someone you know who may have found their right niche in life. What about their calling and contribution is visible to you, and how do you feel about it?

CHAPTER 3

Doorways to Calling

The breeze at dawn has secrets to tell you
Don't go back to sleep

You must ask for what you really want
Don't go back to sleep

People are going back and forth across the doorsill
Where the two worlds touch

The door is round and open
Don't go back to sleep.

—From Essential Rumi
Translated by Coleman Barks

I BELIEVE WE ARE ALL BORN TO A CALLING, specifically to our own calling. Never mind that it may express itself in several different forms throughout our lives. We all have special and unique gifts. We all enter this world through a big door labeled **BORN TO EXPRESS YOURSELF**.

In childhood, some of us are lucky enough to have had our gifts acknowledged, encouraged, and nurtured. Unfortunately, many of us did not. Whatever our experience in childhood, when we enter the journey of life, we all have the same questions to answer, sooner or later: "Who am I? And what am I supposed to do here?"

Well, here we are: sooner, or later. You are now presented with a chance to ponder if or how you have already answered those life questions, and how you may want to answer them in the future. I have observed that folks have come to consciousness about their own right work in different ways. For the purpose of providing a framework for your own reflection, I offer here several different doorways to calling consciousness. You may have been aware of cracking open a window for yourself at different times in your life. Or, sur- prisingly, a door may just have opened for you one day. In any case, the stories of others may prompt some interesting reflections on your own journey.

Yup! That's Me!

This is the label I've chosen for the many who've had almost no struggle with the issue of finding their calling. Practically from birth, they exercised their calling, their soul purpose, their destiny, their niche, either full time or part time, and never had to give it another thought. They simply couldn't help it.

I suspect the prodigious and popular film maker **Steven Spielberg** fits into that category. When accepting the Cecil B. DeMille award for lifetime achievement at the 2009 Golden Globe award celebrations, Spielberg talked about his career having come full circle. At age 6 his father took him to a Cecil B. DeMille blockbuster film and he was forever hooked. He made his first 8-minute adventure film with the existing technology at age 12 and never stopped. Now at age 63, after directing some of the most compelling films of our era, he was receiving the award named in honor of the director of his initial career inspiration. And, like others in this category, he may slow down, or shift gears, but I doubt he will ever retire from his calling.

Tom Bergeron, multi-talented and popular host of many TV reality shows, among them my favorite, *Dancing with the Stars*, hosted his first radio show in high school. When asked how long he had been hosting as a profes- sion, he responded with the easy humor that defines his style, "I had my first gig as a fetus."

Many more enter through **Yup! That's Me!**, but for one reason or another, their acknowledged calling remains a passionate avocation, exercised on a part-time basis. It's what they feel compelled to do in order to be whole, in addition to the income-producing activities by which they support them- selves and their families.

My elementary school classmate, **Mary Ann (Buckhout) Wordsworth**, was the acknowledged class artist every year from K to 8 when we shared a classroom. I sat across from her in 8th grade and watched her doodle and draw, draw and doodle all day long, whenever there wasn't a requirement for another use for the pencil. After high school, she and her husband supported their growing family with more steady sources of income. She was the administrative assistant for the Spiritual Life Center at our local college, and her husband was a supervisor with our town's electric light board. Mary Ann admits that early years with the family and her other interest, singing, took priority over painting. When she spontaneously enrolled in a painting class in midlife, she thought "she had died and gone to heaven." From then on, she never stopped drawing and painting, taking art classes and ultimately teaching them. Upon my retirement and return to my hometown in western Massachusetts, there she was, locally renowned. Her landscape watercolors were exhibited with frequency across the entire Pioneer Valley. I am now thrilled to have four memorable scenes of my childhood gracing my living room wall.

My brother Bruce fits this category, too. A talented musician, he found ways throughout his life to play guitar, sing, lead music groups, and teach music. He always exercised this "love" around his fulltime positions from age 18 to the present. He earned his living in one way. He gave himself and others joy in another. I am convinced he'll still be the musical entertainment in some retirement home, making all those around him tap their feet and clap their hands until his very last breath.

I Never Really Thought About It—Until...

This label refers to those who had been circling around their calling but had never connected the dots. With a little probing, their core purpose became clear.

My friend Linda, 65, when faced with the opportunity for a "calling conversation" I initiated during a friendly potluck supper, responded emphatically: "I don't know what my calling is. I don't think I have one." A professionally successful woman who has now retired, she had never posed the question as to the essence of her life and work. And she had never particularly experienced "loving" her jobs, though she did them well. During the conversation about what she did love and do well, she focused on the word "keeper" as being core to her being. Another word was "mother." The concepts of keeper and "mother/nurturer," despite having had no children, were large over her lifetime. She had been, and still was in retirement, the keeper of confidences, the keeper of the vision of any organization in which she worked or belonged, the protector of an organization's fundamental community, nurturer of the health and happiness of her many staff, the keeper of the books. She was the go-to person, the informal leader of just about everything of which she was a part.

Upon leaving our gathering, this was one happy woman. The dots connected, her life was starting to make sense to her, and she was ready to initiate "calling conversations" with her many friends. I was again pleased at how meaningful these conversations are. She was delighted that her new-found calling cognizance seemed to give her a special appreciation of her essential value to the world, and a willingness to more consciously employ her gifts throughout her retirement.

My friend Evelyn was similar. She had also been a bit intimidated by the concept of "calling." At one point in her life, she toyed with the idea of doing something "more important" than she was doing, and signed up for a short course on "How To Be a World Changer." Her epiphany was that she was already changing the world with her gifts and passion for being an extraordinarily compassionate adult in children's lives. She was an effective and loving parent to three now-grown children and a constant grandparent presence to their four progeny.

I have enormous respect for those who consciously choose this parenting role with gusto. I'm sad that a calling of conscious parenting—a contribution of such enormity—is so often undervalued. In addition to the major time demands of that parenting/grandparenting role, my friend Evelyn still owns and operates Valley Mill, a children's camp in Maryland, which is guided by the principles of appreciation, encouragement and attention in age-appropriate developmental activities—the same qualities she exhibited as a parent of three. She's an ordinary person whose extraordinary lifetime gifts and passions are extremely visible to, and of benefit to, her friends and family.

Following Your Nose

This category is an entry point for people who have been open to many different experiences. They try out lots of jobs, volunteer activities, assignments, colleges and college courses. They take the next steps that seem to open for them. Along the way they may or may not notice what they are good at, and what excites them. Nevertheless, while they journey through life, they are building knowledge and skills and honing their interests. One day they find themselves saying, "Somehow, everything I've ever done has led me here. I think I've found my niche."

Peg Wilson Taylor used these exact words with me after reading one of the early drafts of this manuscript. She never dreamed that one day she would start a small community college in the hills of Kentucky as a branch of the University of Kentucky. She saw it as her crowning achievement, her most fulfilling work, and a magnificent contribution.

Peg and I reconnected at our 50th high school reunion. She had grown up in the Connecticut suburbs, gone to Indiana University, married, raised two children and planned to teach at the high school level. Life happened. She and her husband moved from the University of Connecticut to the University of Kentucky in Lexington. Following their divorce, Peg taught freshman composition at the University and found herself in a doctoral program studying how people learn. She also found herself recruited to teach study skills for the University's Counseling Center.

After eight years as a single mom, she remarried a professor of agronomy and moved to his county of origin, McCreary County in the foothills of the Cumberlands. Given an opportunity to take a sabbatical from the University and aware that high school students needed learning skills before they went to college, Peg traveled to school systems in southeastern Kentucky sharing her growing expertise in learning skills.

Meanwhile, in her new home county, civic leaders wanted to establish a local community college campus. Peg's connections to the University of Kentucky, paired with her vision of the needs of students in rural areas, led to her being chosen to lead the effort to establish the college and campus. Her accumulated experience, her connections, and her nose for challenge opened the door. She says "she married into" the county and its culture and, through enlightened self-interest, followed her nose until her appointment as founder and first president of Somerset Community College/McCreary Center. Now in retirement, she operates a unique bed and breakfast on her small, secluded and peaceful farm bordering Daniel Boone National Forest lands. **Visit www.farmhouseinnbb.com.**

The Wounded...

This is a doorway to calling that many will recognize. Those who enter here operate in fields of endeavor close to their callings for much of their lives, trying to figure out why they were placed on the planet and how they could heal their own deep wounds. Consciously or unconsciously, they feel an urgent need to make sense of their own lives and to keep others from being wounded in similar ways. Finally, through struggle and pain they create a life that coalesces into something *they* love—something that works for themselves and for others. Typically they will admit: "My struggles and my pain are what have brought me to a place of fulfillment."

I read about **Delores** in the newspaper. She'd had a devastating relationship with money for many years: she was constantly in debt, had been evicted from her home, and continually struggled to get her life in order. Finally, with help, the fog lifted. Over a period of years, she got her degree in finance, cleaned up her personal mess, and began teaching others how to relate to money in a constructive way. This became the love of her life: she worked with clients, volunteered in prisons, community centers, and banks. Her passion was to help others become capable enough to address their own devastating realities; work their ways to financial freedom; and become productive members of society.

Those who come to their calling through the door marked **The Wounded** are those whose gifts to the world are built on hard-won survival and healing strategies which have allowed them to master their craft from many perspectives, and to be of service to special populations in special ways. They are often our most credible teachers, an example being former gang leaders who are so tremendously effective at getting young delinquents off the streets and more productively engaged.

I have always considered myself one of those wounded. My mother was a person of great gifts. However, I suffered, along with several of my siblings, in our relationships with her. She tended to think in black and white, knew what was right, and either didn't listen to or understand the more nuanced ways that I made sense of the world. Sadly, I concluded I was the one who was unacceptable and not worthy. I spent a good part of my early professional years trying to figure out the path that was to be mine.

Finally, a series of epiphanies occurred when I started noticing that no matter what I did in my variety of teaching roles, my specialty was always the same. I asked questions, listened deeply to others, helped them trust their own knowing and encouraged them to act on their own wisdom, providing the kind of support I had so yearned for in my formative years.

This seemed to be the station in life I loved the most, where I was most gifted, and where I seemed to be able to serve others well. It was a kind of coaching, before coaching became the profession it is today. At mid-life, as I worked to do more and more coaching of groups and individuals, my career and my calling happily meshed into one and the same.

It Just Came and Got Me!

This was how **Barbara Perman** described the way she and her calling connected in 1996. Disillusioned with the field of education, she had resigned her teaching responsibilities and surrendered to the idea that the next steps would show themselves in the right time and in the right way. At the same time, her elderly mother was about to remarry and relocate. Her mother faced the almost insurmountable task of downsizing, selling her beloved home of 48 years, and moving to the next phase of her life. For four months, Barbara used the time and mental space she had to "volunteer" to help her mother through the process of deciding what to keep, what to dispose of, and which threads of her life she wanted to weave into the tapestry of her remaining years. Instead of the dreaded experience Barbara had anticipated, the time she spent with her mother turned into a rare opportunity that ultimately strengthened their bond.

"After Mom was settled," Barbara recalls, "I realized that other people must need this kind of help. I understood at that moment that I didn't have to resume my search for employment. A new profession had actually found me!" Barbara's epiphany led her to create a professional consultancy in 1996.

She established Moving Mentor Inc., a business focused on helping elders and their adult children through the moving process.

In 2003, the local newspaper called her "the diva of downsizing." Moving Mentor, Inc. offers a range of hands-on services, as well as self-help tools and checklists to ease the transition. Hers was one of the first companies to do this kind of work, and was an early member of The National Association for Senior Move Managers. **Visit www.movingmentor.com.** For the national association, **visit www.nasmm.org**.

Something is Really, Really Wrong with this Picture...!

Finally, there are those who encounter their calling propelled by an angst that something is out of kilter, something needs to be done, and they have skills to address what's off. Here, I extrapolate from the website of **Chris Martenson**, who was a highly successful 40-year-old vice president and strategic consultant for a Fortune 300 company. Although his first love was science and teaching and he earned his Ph.D in neurotoxicology, he decided that college teaching would not be a good fit with other things he wanted to do in life. So, he went on to get his degree in finance, entered corporate life, and made his fortune.

But his talent and love for scientific research, analysis, and teaching never left him. Rather, they conspired to organize themselves differently and uniquely. His intuition told him something was not right with the world of economics, energy and the environment. He proceeded to gather data, test hypotheses and seek to learn why he felt so discomforted about our national and international situation. Finally satisfying his own need to understand, he concluded that most people did not comprehend how money works, and thus were not properly preparing themselves for the future.

At the age of 45, Chris made some changes. He moved his family from their comfortable home in suburban Connecticut to rural western Massachusetts, where he could establish a more self-sufficient lifestyle. He also set about sharing what he has concluded about our economic situation through a PBS Special and a free online program entitled THE CRASH COURSE. Go to his website and experience the clarity of the calling to which he is devoting the rest of his life—basically explaining the complexities of our financial system to the rest of us, and inviting us to consider new choices based on the understanding we gain. He's a man deeply committed to his calling to make his fellow citizens more financially literate in these times of economic uncertainty. **Visit www.chrismartenson.com.**

Wounded Healer and Something is Really, Really Wrong were the two doors that **Dr. John Fisher** had to discover and walk through. He emerged as a whole being, exercising a powerful life of calling and contribution. I first met John on a pilgrimage to Greece in 2006, led by pioneering psychotherapist and author Ed Tick (War and the Soul, 2005). As a 60-year-old chiropractor and Vietnam combat veteran, John was seeking ways to heal himself from years of PTSD-sourced debilitating flashbacks, nightmares, and the resulting destruction of two marriages. For more than 30 years, he had engaged in many attempts to relieve his demons.

There were significant healings on that trip, among them John's. After several rituals were performed on Athenian battle grounds, he began to understand his emotional pain. He made peace with his life as a warrior for his country and met the leading lady of his life to be. He has since retired from full-time chiropractic practice, moved across the country, and delivers Ed Tick's powerfully healing Soldier's Heart seminars to returned veterans. Because there is clearly so much wrong with the way combat vets are welcomed home, he now makes annual trips to Vietnam for healing missions. He escorts health teams and former warriors, bringing to vets on both sides of the war the healing that only heartfelt forgiveness and genuine service can bring. He is a moving speaker, author, and healer to the war-weary. Thankfully, he's found his place. **Visit www.johnwesleyfisher.com.**

What's Next for Me?

If you recognize yourself as entering calling consciousness through one of these doorways, congratulations! If you have not resonated with any of the above, perhaps you are parked on the other side of the door called **What's Next for Me?** Welcome! If you have been waiting in the wings, just hoping for someone or something to push the door open for you, perhaps you are ready to risk discovering what you love, and doing more of it in your life—right here and right now.

If you are at the beginning of your working life, you may want to explore the possibilities of, and set your intention for, having a deeply satisfying and meaningful profession. Those in the middle of working years may be ready to focus squarely on what matters to them with the question: "How do I really want to spend my time for the rest of my life?" Those like myself who are in retirement may want to reflect and remind themselves what gifts they still have to give and the kind of legacy they would like to leave behind. At whatever age, your passion can be fully tapped, and that brings us to our next series of possibilities.

Reflection

How do friends who are exercising their calling describe the way they found themselves?

Which of the doorways provided you with a way to contemplate your own calling?

What are the parts of your calling that you can begin to name?

Whom do you know who could help you learn more about doing what you love?

CHAPTER 4

Passion is Welcome—At Any Age

"Stay foolish....Stay hungry."
—*Stewart Brand*

I AM ENTRANCED BY THOSE ELDERS who, in their 60's and 70's, choose to extend their passion into retirement. Perhaps they are simply transforming the ways in which they share what they love, in an effort to keep themselves alive, well and happy.

I was particularly taken with Red Sox fan Mel Springer, 72, and his wife Alice, who delighted an audience of elders recently at a retirement community program I attended. This was one of 30 "gigs" they had scheduled for the summer, and Mel introduced himself by saying, "I have two passions—baseball and music. I hope you'll enjoy my indulging in both of them with you."

In 1999, at the age of 65, Mel and co-author Ty Waterman wrote a well-researched period book about their favorite team: *The Year The Red Sox Won The Series: A Chronicle of the 1918 Championship Season.* Mel shared his enthusiasm about Massachusetts baseball history and lore—and, as he was also a jazz pianist and former teacher at the New England Conservatory, he proceeded to engage the audience in a rousing sing-a-long with tunes of the '20s and '30s. Our time with this passionate man was both informative and FUN! Once again, I concluded: It is never too late to find meaning, offer unique expertise, and make enlivening choices in the remaining years of one's life.

And passion at any age can attract the financing needed to put your dreams to work. I received a letter from an old friend, David Patton, now 70, with whom I'd had the privilege of traveling to Bali in the 1980's. David has had a lifelong commitment to the Balinese people, and he has a deep respect for the spiritual cultures of the world. In his letter, David wrote that he was seeking financial support for the Lontar Project, an effort aimed at teaching young people the ancient ways of carving the stories of their culture onto palm leaves.

The cultural crisis that drew him to this effort is a current one. The ancient Balinese scrolls are disintegrating, and few older, skilled craftsmen remain to replace them. David is collaborating with the Balinese people to preserve the culture by creating the very first Lontar public library on the island of Bali.

I eagerly contributed a small amount of money, both to support this good cause and to encourage my friend's passion to make a difference. David reports that, over the last year, 56 beautiful palm leaf Lontar have been completed by young scribes, and that the project has thrilled the local sponsors— along with providing paid work for Balinese. (For further information about his progress, you can **email David at www.oghama@ninegates.org**.)

Another resource for funding your passion is the Internet. Tom Adams, 43, a creative videographer, musician, cartoonist, and web designer, operates a site called Reelife Productions (**www.reelifeproductions.com**). Tom is reclaiming a passion that began 17 years ago, when he shot interview footage of the band Phish during their formative years. Marriage and the beginning of a family moved his project to a back burner for several years. But the idea of creating of a full-length feature documentary about his once favorite band never lost its place on his long-term dream list. Now middle-aged, Tom wants to document the maturing of the band for their equally maturing and still loyal fan base.

Social networking and associated technologies will help make his dream possible. Tom discovered Kickstarter.com, where pledges can be solicited for projects which appeal to one's friends as well as to anyone else who happens upon the invitation. These pledges will not be cashed in until the needed amount is pledged, thereby guaranteeing the project. "I'm convinced that harnessing the power of the Internet to reach out to the vast number of fellow Phish phans located around the globe is the only way this lonely— hearted independent producer is going to finally get to produce this film," says Tom in his solicitation. Though not a Phish phan myself, I remain a diehard supporter of friends who choose to live their dreams with passion. I pledged a small amount to signal my support and best wishes.

(Sadly, at the time of going to press, the necessary support for this project had not arrived by the stipulated deadline. I do know that this energetic man will find a way to do this, somehow, sometime.)

And not to leave out the younger generation, I particularly applaud those in their teens and 20s who are daring to get an early start on their passionate commitments. The more people start out life seeking jobs that truly fulfill them, the healthier our society will be. I am hopeful.

In the surrounding towns, there are five colleges and ten high schools. As might be expected, the 2009 graduation ceremonies all produced passionate exhortations for living well—both from students and from internationally renowned speakers. Among them was 2009 Amherst Regional High School Valedictorian Keri Lambert, 18, who urged her fellow graduates to be engaged: "Death doesn't occur when the heart stops beating, it's when the heart stops feeling."

And "feeling" is part of what it takes to contribute something meaningful. I heartily applaud all the younger comrades who give earnest attention to their values, their calling, and the nature of the contributions to which they aspire, at the very beginning of their professional lives. And there are a special few, whose gift is to invite their peers into conversations about calling. As an example, let me tell you about Angela Lussier, 28.

On entering my local library one day, I noted a flyer on the door with the picture of a young woman. She was offering a series of eight free classes on ways to find the work you love. The flyer itself was magnetic, compelling, exciting. It exuded the scent of "calling." I surmised, "Here is a woman who is just starting her practice, and she has already found her right work. I'm going to stop in and see if my assumption is correct."

The next day, I returned to join the class. Angela was holding forth before her much older audience, answering their questions with a confidence and professionalism that belied her years. I stayed afterwards to learn more about her story. "This is only my second month in business for myself," she admitted to me with a slightly embarrassed chuckle. I admitted to her my intrigue with those who are exercising their calling in the world, and my sense that she had found hers. And the gates opened:

"Yes, absolutely! After college, one of my positions was with a recruiting company. I had a hard time making my placement numbers. My bosses were annoyed. I couldn't face putting round people into square job slots for which I knew they might have been qualified—but which weren't a good fit. My efforts to help the job seekers conflicted with the company's goal of filling the slots. It was clear I had to leave. And then I lucked out: I attended a weekend workshop where the organizing question was, 'When you get up each morning to go to work, are you going to a job, to your career, or to your calling?' WOW!"

She continued: "I saw my situation for what it was. By an accident of fate, I had found my 'right work,' and I needed to be doing it. What I've noticed is that since I decided to pay attention to what is my work, everything is falling into place, kind of miraculously—with very little effort on my part." And then she concluded with a statement I frequently hear from those who find their right work: "I guess that's the way it is when you are doing what you are supposed to be doing on the planet."

This young woman was, in her words, "having a blast." Her only worry was that she might be a little young to be taken seriously by her clients. It was clear to me that her courage would soon pay off. In her case, trusting her passion and her abundant expertise was a good call. I invite readers to her fabulous website and blog: **www.my365degrees.com**.

Yes, I am pleased to encounter elders still sharing their passions. And I am hopeful for the younger generation. I do believe it might be easier and more possible for them to activate their passions at an earlier age than was common when I was growing up:

- Perhaps because success is being more broadly defined these days—beyond cars, boats, swimming pools, and money in the bank. It seems to matter more that we do something in life that matters to us.

- Perhaps because it is becoming quite clear that more money cannot buy happiness.

- Perhaps because, with the world being smaller and technological capability being greater, information abounds from worldwide sources about needs, options, models and possibilities. Nearly every young person is computer-literate.

- Perhaps the uncertain economics of the times and the unfortunate consequences of questionable corporate practices have stimulated consideration of new pathways to livelihood. As jobs become scarcer and the usual path to corporate life become a less sure and less worthy route to success, doing what you love becomes a more viable option.

But no matter one's age, those who choose to pursue their passions tend to be those who walk lightly on the planet, adding to, rather than draining energy from their friends and co-workers. I am not a baseball fan, I don't follow rock bands, and I'm not very adept with new technologies. But I am always excited when someone shows up with a passionate interest in some endeavor or other. Those people give me hope that we could enjoy being together and learning together in communities of work and play. They give me hope that our lives can be more connected, more healthy and more happy. They inspire me to wonder: If we lived together as like-minded passionistas in our organizations and our communities, are there any limits to what we could do?

ADDITIONAL RESOURCES YOU MAY ENJOY

What's Age Got to Do With It? Secrets to Aging in Extraordinary Ways by Kelly Ferrin, gerontologist, 1999. Volume II 2009.

Animal, Vegetable, Miracle by Barbara Kingsolver, 2008 One family lives off the land for a year and learns to feed themselves in many ways.

CHAPTER 5

❧

The Possible Organization

"Throughout the centuries there were people who took first steps down
new roads armed with nothing but their own vision."
—*Ayn Rand*

SO WHAT ABOUT THOSE PASSIONISTAS who gather together with a
leader who can unite them into one mission? Is there such a thing as a "do
what you love" organization? I was surprised and pleased to find out there is!
While on a short vacation out of state, I fell, and severely injured my shoulder. Always extremely healthy and obsessively independent, I was catapulted
into a world I had rarely visited, which happened to be populated by people,
almost all of whom, as far as I could tell, were doing what they loved.

Across six weeks, I was cared for by three institutions whose employees
and caretakers seemed universally to be doing what they loved, each and
every day. I found myself continually amazed and delighted, and I give them
credit for the positive attitude I was able to maintain despite being completely
homebound for about six weeks. I applaud them publicly now.

The first institution was Maine Medical Center in Portland, Maine. As I
was leaving in a wheelchair, the youthful aide assisting me asked (as if I were
leaving a hotel), "And how was your stay here?" I replied that I had been
astonished at the quality of every interaction over my two nights, beginning
with the emergency room. I queried him: "Does everyone here do what they
love? Do you do what you love?" The young man said, "Yes." He said his
father had taught him early on that doing what you are called to do was
worth far more than doing something for the money.

I pursued my inquiry. "How is it that every interaction was so great?"
"Well, several things," he replied. "Our president is great. He sets the tone.
And, you were fortunate. In any organization, you will run into colleagues

who are not a good fit for their work. But here, there are very few. We seem to weed them out quickly."

As I graduated to Health South Acute Rehabilitation Facility in Ludlow, Massachusetts, for the next 10 days, I was surprised to encounter a similar atmosphere. How could such a complex staffing system provide the quality and compassion and coordinated 24/7 care I required, given that I was unable to do much of anything for myself? Appreciating how hard both the work and the coordination was, I would occasionally ask a nurse or an aide or a physical or occupational therapist about their tenure and whether they liked the work. The answers were always similar. "I've been here a long time and this is the work I love."

Wherever I go, my lens as a former organizational consultant is always in place. I couldn't help noting that the atmosphere from the halls never wafted discord or discouragement. The staff had pretty much been there forever; they loved their work; they respected their colleagues; and they took problems in stride. They even graciously and cooperatively flexed their "rules" when faced with my somewhat unusual dietary requests.

After 10 days, I was discharged to my home, admittedly earlier than I felt ready. My ever-loyal handyman was waiting for me with new handrails and a way to raise the couch six inches. Likewise, the Visiting Nurse Association of Holyoke, Massachusetts quickly dispatched on schedule compassionate, competent physical therapists, occupational therapists and shower assistants. Each of those professional caretakers had also entered a career they loved, and seemed nourished by their contributions to their clients—to such an extent that it crossed my mind to change the beneficiaries in my will.

I was telling a friend about this triple-whammy experience and he said: "Martha, this is just too rosy. You are not factoring in that organizations populated by nursing and helping types are those that attract some of our most caring and committed. And it is always easy to serve such an appreciative patient such as yourself."

Yes, that is true. Including the fact that I am upbeat and appreciative and motivated to recover—probably a very good patient. However, given that my hospital roommate was an even older and sicker woman with chronic pain, my conclusions also took into account daily observations of a caring staff who were challenged on an hourly basis by this particular patient. I stand by my conclusions, and still have the warm glow to show for it.

For two weeks, this independent soul, who hardly ever allowed anyone else to care for her, surrendered to necessity and lived, ate, slept, and went to rehab class with the assistance of happy and satisfied service providers. For four more weeks, I was homebound, enjoying meals on wheels from my local senior center, and gratefully accepting the services of the Visiting Nurse Association (VNA). I found that being around those who were joyfully living their calling was personally transforming. I honor them with these words and hope that their standard will set the measure for what is possible in any organization.

One question remains. If it's possible for organizations to be filled with people living in their own right livelihoods, why are there not more of them? Although the health care profession may naturally attract those with a real calling for it, my guess is that the pervasive healthy and happy organizational tone that I experienced has much to do with leadership—a leadership comprised of a robust vision, a sense of possibility, and the daily habits and behaviors that live up to that possibility.

During the time I was homebound, I came across an account of exactly the kind of leadership philosophy that could deliver the organizations described above. In 1970, a citizens committee outside of Philadelphia incorporated the non-profit Resources for Human Development (RHD). They embarked upon an experiment to create and lead a values-based social service organization. It was funded with an initial grant of $50,000. Thirty-six years later, with the same leader and a consistently supportive and visionary board, the organization now serves clients in 14 states and grosses $162,000,000. Their experiment paid off in an extraordinarily profitable testament to the reality that doing good and doing well can co-exist for the benefit of all everyone involved (funding sources, clients, client communities, employees, and the planet on which we live). Fortunately, they wrote about it.

Visionary leader (or chief experimenter, as he might prefer to be called) Robert Fishman, and his wife Barbara Fishman, also an RHD executive, co-authored the story of their organization in their 2006 book, *The Common Good Corporation: The Experiment Worked!*

The seeds of Bob's "calling" were planted early in life, as he reports in a personal statement inaugurating the book. As a young boy, he listened to his parents quarrel repeatedly, and tried to understand why they fought. Carrying that quest through college and graduate school in psychology and social work, he found himself studying hostile relationships, but encountered no professor who had a vision of what a healthy human relationship looked like. In the workplace, he found supervisors with different approaches, but each assumed they were "right" and others were wrong. Reflecting on his personal history and lifelong quest, Bob states: *"RHD was conceived as an experiment. Thirty-six years later, I'm clear that the experiment is about creating healthy workplace communities.... I have come to believe that if human beings want to, they can settle almost every disagreement, but only in one time and in one place. That is what it is like to live in a world of infinite possibility."*

Bob continues: *"Add to this a set of values-based guidelines that small groups can use to manage their conflicts and we are well on the road to a common good corporate effort, with all the energy and creativity that such an effort releases.... I ask you [my readers] to join me as we develop this new corporate form."*

In her own inaugurating statement, Barbara Fishman briefly tracks the rise of the values-blind corporate power we find today. She notes the groundswell of objections beginning to be voiced across the country and around the world. She issues the call: It is our generation that must *"address the lack of values-based behavior...and reshape the corporation for socially responsible ends."*

The common good corporation holds as assumptions three basic values:
- People are of equal human worth
- People are essentially good unless proven otherwise
- There is no single way to manage corporate issues well

It is that last assumption that warmed my heart, given my habitual frustration with all-encompassing and alienating organizational rules that ignore the common sense inherent in the specifics of the local situation. Those same rules, when applied without common sense, often have the effect of running counter to the organization's stated mission of service.

The Common Good Corporation, Bob Fishman's life work, is a treasure chest of ideas, guidelines, and narratives about real-life events that occurred as these assumptions were tested, refined, and applied in RHD. The proof is in the pudding. Personal satisfaction, the common good, and economic success can co-exist as a triple bottom line. $162,000,000, well-served clients, and energetic and creative employees are stunning results. Every organizational leader should read this book, over and over again. **Visit www.commongood-corporation.org.**

ADDITIONAL RESOURCES YOU MAY ENJOY

Instructions to the Cook: A Zen Master's Lessons in Living a Life that Matters by Bernard Glassman and Rick Fields, 1997. This inspirational book documents the founding of Greyston Bakery in Yonkers, New York, in 1982 by Roshi Bernie Glassman. The Greyston Model has since become a "best practice" example of social enterprise and is studied in major U.S. business schools, including Harvard, Yale, Princeton, Stanford University, and New York University. **Visit www.zenpeacemakers.com** to learn more about the calling and life work of socially engaged Buddhism in the United States, based in Montague, Massachusetts.

The Green Collar Economy by Van Jones, 2008. This man's life-work and his common-sense approach posits that the solution to our environmental problems and the widening social gap between the rich and the poor can be addressed by matching the large amount work that needs to be done to increase energy efficiency with the large number of people seeking jobs to lift them out of poverty. **Visit www.greenforall.org** to learn about the new coalitions that leverage public and private investment to create quality green jobs.

CHAPTER 6

Multiply Impact

*"Business has become, in the last half century, the most powerful
institution on the planet. The dominant institution in any society needs
to take responsibility for the whole—as the church did in the days of the
Holy Roman Empire. But business has not had such a tradition.
This is a new role, not yet understood and accepted."*
—*Willis Harmon, August 1990*
Co-Founder, World Business Academy

EVEN A VERY SMALL BUSINESS CAN ORGANIZE ITSELF to meet
multiple bottom-line considerations. The current impetus to green the planet,
steward resources, build community and become socially responsible, all
while being profitable, seems to be driving young and passionate people to
use their gifts to meet deeper needs in our society. As these passionistas begin
to do good and do well, perhaps they will show the rest of the world how
committed communities of good practice can work for all stakeholders.

Erin Kelly-Dill, 39, didn't intend to go into business. It was accidental.
An art history major and lover of sewing, Erin was living in a very rural part
of Western Massachusetts with her husband and three children. She spent
several years casting about trying many jobs—working for a manufacturer of
bike and ski clothing, producing her own line of baby clothes as Dill Pickle,
waitressing, and baking. Creative sewing seemed to be the constant "call"
in her life.

But it was the daily routine of making her three children's lunches, and
filling those plastic sandwich bags day after day (500 a year) that got Erin
thinking. Could she use her love for sewing, have some creative fun, and keep
those plastic bags out of the landfill? In 2003, she created a product called
HappySacks. Her reusable and attractive envelopes for snacks and sandwiches

were a hit with family and friends. She found that local stores were eager to stock the inexpensive, eco-sensitive, and useful product.

Now going by the name of "Snack Taxi," Erin's product moved outside of the region through word of mouth. Serendipitous media coverage enticed many more retail establishments to carry her product, including an eco store in Chicago.

The miracle that every author or business person yearns for happened. The Chicago store, A Cooler Planet, was right around the corner from Oprah Winfrey's headquarters, and frequented by many of her staff for their personal purchases. An Oprah show celebrating Earth Day 2009 featured staff picks for inexpensive "green" products, and Snack Taxi was one of them.

Sales spiked! Other retail stores and online retailers like Nubius Organics wanted to carry Snack Taxi. And why not? It's:

- PVC-free
- An easy way to replace thousands of plastic baggies
- A great addition to your waste-free lunch kit
- Washing machine and dishwasher safe
- Made in the USA

What I appreciated about Erin Kelly-Dill is her basic connection to simple living with her family in a rural area. And I admired her advocacy of social responsibility in business. What that means to me is that everyone involved wins—all stakeholder needs are addressed. Her profit is solid, her clients are satisfied, her employees are happy and fairly treated, and her product is compatible with best environmental practices. Everyone has "enough."

Erin's website is simple, concise, and clear, and it reflects her commitment to producing a useful enviro-friendly product, while keeping her business local. During tough economic times in the hills of western Massachusetts, this is a critical contribution to her neighborhood. At this writing, Erin provides jobs for ten of her talented seamstress neighbors, either full-time with benefits or part-time with pro-rated benefits. Her workroom is a very happy place to be. Kudos to the still happy and fulfilled Erin Kelly-Dill after 6 years in business. **Visit www.snacktaxi.com.**

It's really a very small step from doing what you love in order to keep your self and your family healthy and sane, to doing it and serving those hungry others in your wider community as well. The days of paying attention to a single business bottom line need to be days of the past. That becomes nowhere more obvious than when we consider, in our next chapter, the gifts and contributions of a man who takes the ideas of fairness and justice in business very seriously and applies them on the world stage.

ADDITIONAL RESOURCES YOU MAY ENJOY

Deep Economy: The Wealth of Communities and the Durable Future by Bill McKibben, 2007. This book makes the case for moving beyond "growth" as the paramount economic ideal and pursuing prosperity more locally, with regions producing more of their own food, generating more of their own energy, and even creating more of their own culture and entertainment.

Tyranny of the Bottom Line: Why Corporations Make Good People Do Bad Things by Ralph Estes, 1995. Not his most recent book, but one that illuminates the dangers of the one-dimensional focus on the single bottom line of corporate profit.

YES! a magazine which supports people worldwide in building a just, sustainable, and compassionate world. Compiles powerful ideas and practical actions from around the world. **Visit www.yesmagazine.org.**

CHAPTER 7

❧

Change the System

"Never believe that a few caring people can't change the world.
For, indeed, they are the only ones who ever have."
—*Margaret Mead*

SOCIAL RESPONSIBILITY HAS MANY FACES. It is definitely a common and well regarded practice for individuals to volunteer their time to community organizations—all the better if they are giving what they are good at and love to do. For instance, every community over the years has had their share of outstanding Boy and Girl Scout leaders who transform the lives of kids and love every minute of it.

It is also a long-standing practice for church members and social groups to consider it their joyful obligation to help their communities by funding scholarships, sponsoring sports teams, and running food drives. Local businesses in particular also understand that partnering with local causes and offering pro bono services of all kinds brings them good will from their local patrons, while nourishing the community in which they operate. Charity, too, has been a long-standing vehicle for promoting the health and well-being of the less fortunate.

As other options emerge for helping those in need, charitable efforts are under more scrutiny by those in the business community. More and more, we need to find ways to offer the individuals in communities around the globe a future, not just provide the sustenance to get through recurring daily challenges. To quote an oft-recited proverb, *If you give a man a fish, he will eat for a day. If you teach him how to fish, he will eat forever.*

Clearly, there are deep and broad social needs that seek our contributions—needs for security, education, food, health, clean water, economic self sufficiency, women's rights, and self-determination around the globe. People who are most affected by those problems are the ones most motivated to solve them in perpetuity, if given the means. The key is to teach them how to fish. Better yet to work to go one step further and *change the fishing industry* so that it serves everyone involved.

The social entrepreneurs are in business to do just that. They are the relatively new faces in the crowd of the socially responsible. They are passionate to make a difference at the level of any system change that is required to make fairness and justice and viable livelihoods available to all. They recognize existing social problems and use entrepreneurial principles to organize, create, and manage ventures to provide that means and to promote social changes.

Whereas a business entrepreneur typically measures performance in profit and return, a social entrepreneur assesses success in terms of the impact he or she has on society. Where once a business bottom line focused only the profit for stockholders, the concept of multiple bottom lines—profitability, economic justice and fairness, and environmental sustainability—are all standards by which each and every business that calls itself socially responsible is being challenged to measure itself.

While a deeper discussion of social entrepreneurship is beyond the scope of this book, I reference it because the model is so powerful and hopeful for addressing serious issues of system change around the globe. For any reader who may be uncovering or exploring his or her passion for social change, the social entrepreneurship literature, the history, and the principles and projects are worthy of further investigation.

Once again, serendipity struck when it came time to write about the larger venues to which people are called. Something in me said: "You need to go to this meeting on Thursday." It was a moderated discussion of business ethics at which a well-known visionary social entrepreneur was participating. I had known of his reputation for high standards of ethical practice. I hadn't planned on including him in this book, as his obsessions for good works have been well-publicized in other venues. But, for reasons I knew not, I needed to go to that meeting. Sitting in the audience, I was mesmerized and changed my plan.

Dean Cycon, 52, of Leverett, MA, founder of Dean's Beans Organic Coffee, deserves every bit of acknowledgement he gets. After 18 years in a socially responsible business model of his own creation, his passion was too palpable to ignore. I hope his example will inspire other such visionaries/ activists who uncover similar gifts, talents and passions to follow their hearts into the larger arena of actual system change.

In a recorded interview posted on his website, Cycon reported that as a very young man, he knew he was called to work for social justice through environmental issues. He wanted to change the world—not by charitable works, which are a temporary boon, but by changing the systems and assumptions by which the world operates. Thinking that the vehicle for most effectively exercising his passion would be through the law, he went to law school and did his time practicing environmental law with large corporations. But lawyering was not to be his vehicle. It was business—the coffee business, to be exact—that allowed Cycon to develop a business model unique for these times, with an international reach into communities of suppliers from 14 countries, many of them indigenous peoples who do not speak the primary language of their own countries.

Dean Cycon lays out the problem he faced in his book, *Java Trekker*:

"... coffee prices are dictated largely by the forecasts of financial speculators, banks and multinational corporations in New York and London. One month a farmer may receive a reasonable reward for his or her labors, and the very next month the price can plummet."

"......During the first five years of the new millennium, coffee prices were often lower than the cost of production, driving hundreds of thousands of coffee families off their lands and into crowded cities or across borders. Sometimes this forced exodus ended in death, with desperate migrant farmers falling off trains in Mexico or abandoned in locked vans in the Texas heat."

According to Cycon, attempts have been made to create an "ethical pricing system" by Fair Trade and other private and public initiatives. While they have been somewhat successful in keeping thousands of farmers on their lands, those farmers are growing only a small fraction of the world's commercial coffee.

Dean, the man, has made a commitment. He buys 100% fair trade organic coffee. He pays more—sometimes substantially more—to make it fair to all parties, most specifically the indigenous growers from 14 countries which he regularly visits. A percentage of the profits are returned to the communities of the growers to use as they wish to improve the conditions of health and education in the village.

This maverick acknowledges making himself somewhat unpopular by inviting his competitors to do the same. Sadly, one loophole is in the labeling. What do these "good" labels—organic, green, socially responsible, fair trade—mean, product by product? This is not the first time this question has arisen in different product areas. When applied to coffee, does a 10% buy of "fair trade coffee beans," when the percentage is not publicly disclosed, indicate that the company is committing to social justice or is it simply engaging in another version of "cause marketing?"

The founding questions that underlie Dean Cycon's initial experiment and early enthusiasm are still relevant today—for him and for any other businessperson who would like to take them on as their own.

- What could happen if a company took a level of responsibility for the conditions found in the villages it was buying from through direct development work and support to the community?

- Could the dynamics of poverty which seem endemic to coffee growing be challenged and overcome?

- Could the company still be profitable?

The indications after 18 years are positive. There is so much more to this story. I encourage you go to the source: **www.deansbeans.com**.

ADDITIONAL RESOURCES YOU MAY ENJOY

Visit **www.ashoka.org,** the global association of the world's leading social entrepreneurs—men and women with system-changing solutions for the world's most urgent social problems.

JAVATREKKER: Dispatches from the World of Fair Trade Coffee by Dean Cycon, 2007. An adventure story with heart. Visit **www.deansbeans.com** to learn more about the Fair Trade Roadmap and the corporate Comprehensive Sustainability commitments of the company, and lots more.

Ecological Intelligence: How Knowing the Hidden Impacts of What We Buy Can Change Everything by Daniel Goleman, 2009

Visit greenamericatoday.org. Information and resources about how you can participate in changing the world.

Get a Grip: Clarity, Creativity and Courage in a World Gone Mad by Frances Moore Lappe, 2008. A long time social activist and prolific author, Lappe came to prominence in 1971 with her groundbreaking Diet for a Small Planet. Her latest book highlights radical new ways of thinking about fear, power, democracy, and hope itself.

Reflection

You've come to the place where you have been reading and thinking about "calling" and "contribution" and how they might relate to you.

— Get a cup or tea or coffee, find a quiet spot, sit down.

— Appreciate that there is nothing to do right now.

— Take a long, low, deep breath.

We're taking a break for some reflection.

• What struck you as you were reading?

• What feelings did you notice, and about what?

• What questions emerged for you?

• Whom do you know, or see on TV, or read about in the newspaper, who seems to be living in the niche that is totally meant for them?

And, most important...

What's becoming clear to you?

Here, we leave Part One and move into Part Two. So far you have taken some time to consider the nature of calling and contribution through the stories of those who seem to have found the balance of the two for themselves. A few of those you have read about have achieved some renown and acclaim as they burrowed into the expression of their natural gifts and passions. Most are people who have simply given themselves permission to answer a "call," are fulfilled doing what they love, and are enjoying the fact that it matters to

others. For some, the scope of the "contribution" is limited to family; for others, the impact reaches to villages in 14 countries. It is important to remember that fame and fortune is not what this book is about. Neither is it about needing to have a worldwide impact.

The truth, as every teacher knows, is that it is impossible to tell in the moment how the impact of a comment, an assignment, an encouragement, even a criticism will affect lives in the future. When we live authentically, we live authentically. The consequences may not be immediately visible beyond our own sense of personal contentment with being true to ourselves. Thus my hope is that you, the reader, have been able throughout Part One, to open your mind to the possibilities that exist for one who is true to themselves in this world—and that you don't back away from your emerging sense of what is yours to do. That is the point of this book.

As you enter Part Two, you will get a chance to probe more deeply into your own history, your own patterns, your own wants and calls to service. And you can see where that leads you.

PART TWO

Take Time to
Explore Your Truth

TAKE TIME TO EXPLORE YOUR TRUTH

WELCOME TO PART TWO, where you will have the opportunity to more directly explore your own life. Here, you will discover patterns, talents, gifts, and calls to serve, which you can begin to claim as your own.

The questions in the following Part Two chapters invite you to consider how the things you love—your gifts and talents, your desires, and your calls to service—make you a totally unique contributor to the planet. You will have an opportunity to see more clearly where you belong, how you might serve, the changes that matter most deeply to you, and the qualities that make your efforts meaningful, regardless of the result.

- I ask you to temporarily put aside any fear that spending time focusing on yourself, your loves, and your wants is a selfish thing to do.

- I ask you to put aside any need for a quick answer.

- I ask you to be willing to slow down and savor your time with "what's true for you."

As you enter this section, I want to introduce the value of paradox—of being of two minds. There is a kind of targeted goal energy that is useful in keeping you focused and on track. There is also a kind of relaxed awareness—an openness to what's happening—that will allow the process to teach you what you need to do next. Both are equally necessary.

He who asks a question is a fool for five minutes; he who does not ask a question remains a fool forever.

— CHINESE PROVERB —

...Yes, it's important to **stay focused** and proceed with the process as it's laid out...

... and yes, it's important to **meander** and engage in the process the way that is most useful to you.

Hold these apparent opposites as your friends. Both approaches will be useful to you. You can: **Follow the process as it's laid out.** For example, under the question, "What do you want?" you will see a list of related questions. You will also see, sprinkled throughout this book, words like goal, intention, outcome. You will benefit from staying on target, answering the questions in order, and focusing on the assignment given. After all, you are reading this book because you want something different in your life. Certainly you want to do more of what you love. Perhaps you have also come to this process with a strong desire to give back, or to address some of the world's deep failings and needs. Your "will" is engaged to the extent that you are seriously goal-focused on making a change in your life and willing to follow a process to do so.

At the same time, in the spirit of paradox, you can also: **Stay open to discovering how you need to proceed.** Information about your gifts, your talents, your birthright, what you are meant to do on the planet, will surface in its own time, in an atmosphere of safety, trust, and curiosity. The words *invite, allow, receive, listen,* and *meander* come to mind. The information you seek will be less likely to surface under pressure or in desperation. In my opinion, you can't "will" your calling into existence. You can invite it to show itself, and you can welcome it and receive it. You can trust that it will emerge.

Welcoming the "both stances are useful in tandem" approach is your key. Stay focused on the outcomes you want from this process and be open to whatever the process teaches you about how to proceed. Enjoy and utilize the apparent opposites. I urge you to balance any needs for preconceived specific outcomes with lots of reflecting and listening. See what emerges.

There are other ways to think about this same paradox. For instance, we are a culture that prizes efficiency and speed and fast results. We'd like to think that a straight line is the shortest distance between two points. And yet it is only in retrospect when we notice that it is the unanticipated detours in our lives that have allowed us to learn the lessons that will make it possible for us to reach a destination or produce an outcome that rings true for us. It is only in retrospect that a journey diagrammed by "A," followed by "X," then followed by "13," subtract "4," and add "P," is a journey that may actually be the shortest one we could manage to get where we really wanted to go.

Let's add to this notion of paradox the apparent opposites of "toughness" and "gentleness." Neither one will be effective in this process without a good dose of the other. I invite you to be both tough and gentle with yourself as you work with the questions. Here's what I mean:

- Be tough. Commit to start the process and finish it; keep going even when you feel stuck.

- Be gentle. Give yourself permission to answer the questions in any order and way you wish.

- Be tough on yourself: notice the questions you don't want to answer: They may be the very ones you need to sit with.

- Be gentle with yourself: take a break into silence and reflection whenever the mood hits.

- Be tough on yourself: discern whether "stopping" is evidence of an excuse or an avoidance.

- Be gentle with yourself: understand that there are many forms of exploration. There are times when your insights, your answers and your core beliefs will be more accessible to you than at other times. Sometimes, you need to dig deeper; other times, you need to ask a question and let the answers emerge—over days, or weeks, or even months.

One of the prepublication readers of this manuscript in process said: "I'm having a blast answering the questions, but I'm aware of an internal push-pull when I think about beginning to operate in the world with what I've discovered." In my experience, that is true for most people as they grapple with a new clarity about their lives. You might find yourself thinking: "How can I ever get the courage to act on the role I am wanting to play at this point?"

Don't worry. We'll come to the push-pull in Part Four, with three powerful questions which will help you explore those dimensions more deeply. Any tension you feel will be held up to the light of day—where it will lose its mystery and join in conversation with you. If thoughts such as "how will I ever..." begin to overwhelm you, do your best to set them aside until we get to Part Four.

Once again, **be tough** on yourself. If unexpected emotions arise—particularly the unwelcome ones like fear, sadness, anger, embarrassment or shame—acknowledge them, and see what follows. Hold to what feels true, and continue to move along your path.

Once again, **be gentle** on yourself. Invite forward all the emotions that reside within, and hold them with a sense of curiosity and appreciation.

I believe that for most of us, finding our calling is essentially a meandering process. You can't really plan it out in a straight timeline. For many, it is identified only once you have arrived and are operating out of it. People talk about it as, "This is what I was meant to do on the planet."

On the other hand, what you *can* do is to commit yourself to the tasks of uncovering what you love to do, what you are good at, and what you are passionate about. And you can dare to do more of it. Ultimately, with a bit of good luck, all the puzzle pieces of your life converge to where you can ultimately say, "Everything I have done and learned and accomplished made it possible for me to now live and contribute in this very satisfying way."

In the following chapters, your job is to identify and collect the puzzle pieces of your life which have given you the most satisfaction. These are the building blocks with which you can begin to create a life that works for you and which open up more possibilities for you.

First, we'll inquire about your parents and other adult models, and their relationships with calling. Second, we'll review the chronology of your life and seek patterns of passion and activity. Third, we'll ask lots of questions about your interests and desires.

So let's begin!

CHAPTER 8

What's Your Heritage?

"Our greatest responsibility is to be good ancestors."
—Jonas Salk

ONE OF THOSE PUZZLE PIECES is your "calling heritage." As I thought about this particular query, it occurred to me to offer a bit of my own "calling heritage." I hope it will encourage you to mine the rich sources of information and influence in your early life that hold clues for how you think about what's possible for you. I enjoyed reviewing my own story and hope you will be able to find and relish nuggets in your own past. Here we go...

Both of my parents found their natural talents and expressed them in their lives: my mother, Betty, early and most easily; my father, Richard, much later and perhaps after more of a life journey. Both encouraged all their six children to do in life whatever they wished. That was a gift in itself. Raised in the Depression, they could have strenuously concluded that all six of us must train for a "safe and high paying" profession, one that would support us in the tough times that were certain to come again.

But they didn't. My mother, knowing the life she wanted to create, simply followed her own heart from an early age and never looked back. She put herself through college on 10-cent tips during the Depression, training to be a physical education teacher. She entered that career immediately after college at a school for the deaf. Throughout her life with her family, in her community as a volunteer, and ultimately as a full-time teacher in the public school system, she was a consummate physical educator and lover of tennis and camping.

She had a gift. She was deeply committed to health and fitness for all ages, and had fun with it.

Over the years she had the entire elementary school population of the town of South Hadley happily jumping rope to extraordinary skill levels (and, by the way, to fitness). In her 80's she was still teaching others to play ping pong in the senior living community, trying to introduce a healthy activity to her friends and increase her cadre of available competitors. Betty's creativity, energy and enthusiasm for teaching the physical arts was her calling, and she is remembered with fondness, long after her death, as a woman who deeply enriched children's lives.

My father Richard's journey, on the other hand, was more difficult. He went into the family business, a retail book, stationary and toy store, and stayed there for his whole working life. He always regretted not having attended college. Although his income-providing work paid the bills for a family of eight, I believe it was not entirely satisfying to him. He later became involved in his church, and overcame a lifelong shyness by taking a Dale Carnegie course, doing his assignments at home at the dinner table much to the family's amusement. Over the years, one of his gifts of financial analysis proved extremely useful in the family bookstore, in Town Meeting, and in church—all while he ensured a good living for his family.

Ultimately, he became interested in saving important land parcels in our region and protecting them for future generations. He founded a privately funded Conservation Society, which preceded the adoption of a formal Conservation Commission as part of town government. For the last 25 years of his life, his ten-acre Christmas Tree Farm was the annual destination for adults and children seeking to share in the tradition of selecting and cutting down their own tree. Richard is also remembered fondly by all those who knew him.

I'm sure there were many examples of frustration and discouragement among my large number of aunts and uncles. Given that I came of age in the 50's, my elders weren't talking much about their interests, talents, or career fulfillment. Those years were more about all of us fulfilling expectations of our parents, doing our duty, becoming "successful." They were less about personal meaning and satisfaction. They were also the times when gender roles pretty much defined what women and men were to do in life—never mind their interests or talents. In 1963, Betty Friedan's groundbreaking work *The Feminine Mystique* began to unlock the sources of women's depression and frustration from their often isolated role of homemaker. Men, as described in 1956 by William Whyte in his classic *The Organization Man*, were equally constrained, even stultified, by the requirements of career progression in the corporations in which they worked.

In my college years at the end of the 50's, my female peers were aware that they wanted something more than staying at home and raising children. The discussions were frequent and full of anxiety. There were many questions. The answers did not seem that easy. My peers and I were raised in a constraining cultural milieu soon to be widely acknowledged. The 60's revolution began to point out the gender-based and race-based inequities of opportunity and the blind spots of the cultural context in which I and most of my aunts and uncles lived our lives.

It wasn't until another groundbreaking work, *What Color is Your Parachute?* by Richard Nelson Bolles* in 1970, that the profession and practice of career planning was born. It was a novel idea to name talents and interests, and learn to demonstrate how they could be a perfect "fit" with employers' needs, to the benefit of both the job seeker and the hiring organization.

Before I leave my own heritage, one more relative deserves mention, as he never bowed to the cultural constraints of the 40s and 50s by which he was surrounded. His passion for what he loved was so obsessive that he simply had no other choice than to break free of any

---

Forty years later, Bolles still issues the annual Parachute update.
See Appendix A

familial or cultural expectations of the times and follow his heart. It was my father's cousin, Irving Johnson, who lived only a few miles away and who was a regular presence in our home. He turned his burning passion for boating into a livelihood of some renown.

Growing up on the banks of the Connecticut River, he was determined to be a sailor from an early age. He once said that if he had been unable to express this passion, he would have undoubtedly become a juvenile delinquent or worse.

Uncle Irving avoided formal education in favor of boats, boats, boats. He sailed around Cape Horn on a four-masted bark. He worked on a freighter. On a schooner, he met and fell in love with a woman, educated at an elite college, who was traveling on the First Class Deck with her parents. Her parents thought this deckhand with little formal education was not good enough for their daughter. Love triumphed and so did the sailor, who created a unique life on the sea for his wife and two sons on the famed Schooner and then Brigantine "Yankee." They made 7 trips around the world assisted by young adventure-seeking deckhands, including my father on one voyage. Irving and Exy, his wife of 50 years, went on to lecture extensively, co-author eight books, and receive many honors. And for all of his life, he was an extraordinary mentor and model to young people.

I clearly had some good family models for doing what one loves—early or late, and with or without formal education. While it's a treat to have a famous relative, I include Irving's story because I believe his renown was simply the byproduct of a life that was all about, and only about, **his insistence on living his passions.**

I believe there is a place for everyone who dares to honor their own passions and gifts. I encourage you to take time to remember both the positive role models and the discouraging influences in your background. Both affect how much permission you will give yourself to both dream and to follow your dreams as you move through the pages of this book.

Reflection

What did your parents or other relatives love to do?

Did they actually make for themselves a chance to do it? Were they happy in work? In their lives?

What childhood or societal messages did you get about whether or not you could build your livelihood on your passions and gifts?

CHAPTER 9

⤜❧

What Patterns Exist in Your Life?

"Say not, 'I have found the truth,' but rather, 'I have found a truth.'
Say not, 'I have found the path of the soul.' Say rather, 'I have met the soul
walking upon my path.' For the soul walks upon all paths."
—*Kahil Gibran,*

WE COME NOW TO LOOK FOR MORE PUZZLE PIECES by reviewing your own life. What has interested you, inspired you, made you curious, given you tremendous satisfaction? The template below is a simply a memory jogger. It gives you a chance to review your life over time and to notice what you particularly enjoyed doing, or what you were really, really good at. It's not so much a forum for listing memorable events in your life, but rather an opportunity to explore activities or ideas that have captured your attention—and captured it repeatedly.

As a child, you were your natural self, in ways that would show up later in life. If no one watched, and no one shared, and no one encouraged or appreciated your gifts and tendencies, you may not have seen yourself clearly. If teachers or parents or others told you that you "should" be somebody you weren't—and you believed them—you had an even more difficult time seeing yourself clearly and acting on what you saw. That's OK. No matter your age, you were still "doing you": it just needs a little extra persistence to make "you" visible.

So grab a piece of paper and pen or a laptop and start making some notes. As you track the course of your life, you may find yourself leaving blanks during certain years. That's OK. Perhaps the memories will surface later. Or you may wish to ask your parents or close relatives for their recollections. It would not be surprising to hear things like, "When you were little, I could never tear you away from _____," or, "When you were in high school, you came home every day talking about your fascination with _____."

At 82, Bill Gates Jr. wrote a loving memoir, *Showing Up*. In it, he focuses on the people and the lessons in his life. He remembers driving his Cub Scout son, who ultimately founded Microsoft, to different neighborhoods to knock on doors and sell cookies, candy, and other fundraising items. So competitive was the young man, that he annually sold more than any of his peers. Foreshadowing? Quite likely.

Like everyone else on the planet, you have been doing "you" all your life. At each stage in your life, what was your favorite thing to do? In each of your activities, what was your particular way of doing it? (Think Bill Gates III as a competitive cookie sales kid in Cub Scouts.) What purpose did you seem to be living out in each activity?

See what gifts, talents and passions keep surfacing in whatever situation you find yourself—in high school, in hobbies, in jobs. Discover the environments in which you most thrived. Remind yourself of dreams you may have put aside. Write down whatever comes to mind, whether it's something big or something which seems insignificant. Don't overlook the "little things" that occur to you. Allow your mind to offer up whatever clues about how you "do" you that this exercise will invite.

CHILDHOOD
Preschool
Elementary School
Camps, hobbies
Family, trips, relationships, friendships

ADOLESENCE
High School
Camps, hobbies
Family, trips, relationships, friendships
Volunteering

COLLEGE OR TRADE SCHOOL
Courses
Friendships
Volunteering
Part-time work
Internships
Summer jobs

WORKING LIFE POSITION #1
Family & Home
Work assignments
Community volunteering
Hobbies

PARENTING & FAMILY

WORKING LIFE POSITION #2
Family & Home
Work assignments
Community volunteering
Hobbies

WORKING LIFE POSITION #3
Family & home
Work assignments
Community volunteering
Hobbies

WORKING LIFE POSITION #4
Family & home
Work assignments
Community volunteering
Hobbies

WORKING LIFE POSITION #5
Family & home
Work assignments
Community volunteering
Hobbies

Reflection

What patterns seem to surface or repeat themselves
at different times in your life?

What dreams may have been parked in a closet, and
are demanding to see the light of day?

CHAPTER 10

What Matters to Me?

"To be rooted is perhaps the most important and least recognized need of the human soul."
—*Simone Weil*

YOU'VE LAID THE GROUNDWORK by looking at your "calling heritage," and considering their influence on your own path. You've identified those times in your life when you were deeply engaged, curious, passionate—or even obsessed—with something. You may have noticed patterns that had not occurred to you before.

Now we are getting to questions about what really matters to you. I want to take a moment to introduce the questions you will see in the next four chapters, and to suggest how you might work with them.

The questions invite you to articulate what you love, what you are good at, what you want, and how you might be moved to serve. Keep in mind we are not yet looking at how you will make things happen. Rather, we are focusing on what moves you, and why.

I believe that when you focus on what you love, do easily, and care about—with curiosity, courage and commitment—the how-to's will fall into place. The questions in these next four chapters will serve as prompts; they invite you to seek clues about what you may want to offer to the world, in ways that call forth your best, enrich you, and serve others. A win-win for all.

Please understand: the questions are numerous, and they overlap significantly. I do this intentionally, because one or another phrasing may just be the form that elicits your own deep response. So pick and choose, or try them all. And certainly feel free to invent your own.

In this and the following chapters, you will explore four areas:

- What do I love?
- What am I good at?
- What do I want?
- What calls me to service?

As stated, the categories do overlap—and any one of them may trigger your path to self-discovery. Start anywhere. Write down your answers. Ask them over and over: you may get different answers on different days. Let clarity emerge. For some, the information may be ready to flow. For others, the questions may serve as doorways that lead to other doorways that open to deeper wisdom.

Consider the possibility that this may be easier to do with a witness or a helper who knows you, and who can reflect aspects of your personality that you may not see. People frequently do not realize that what they do naturally and as easily as breathing is also unique and valuable. In fact, it is those very effortless, taken-for-granted talents that are at the core of calling. You may need a friend or friends to help you see them.

Here are some approaches that may make the process a bit easier when you get to the actual questions:

1. Answer the version of the question that most calls to you. You may find that a number of questions resonate: if so, go for it!

2. Answer the questions on paper, as a list, at your computer, or with a friend who can take notes.

3. Answer a few questions each day. By taking a daily 15 minutes and repeating the questions and listening for your answers, you are inviting your body and mind to provide insight. By committing to a regular practice for two to four weeks, you put your inner self on notice that you are serious about pursuing this inquiry. You are advising your "deep insides" that you will stay present and listen to any scary or "too big" ideas that may be offered up from that place of your true knowing.

4. Notice any attempt to censor the answers that arise. Park that censorship, at least temporarily! Write EVERYTHING down. After all, you are just thinking freely and listening to yourself. You are not making any decisions or changes yet. You are just exploring your desires, experiences, values and natural talents.

5. Please remember that we're not talking about a job hunt here. We're talking about what matters—to YOU. First and foremost, it's an inside job—an excursion in letting your life talk to you about what you love to do, what you do easily and well, what comes from your heart, what calls forth your best. Once you have a clear sense of your natural and joyous skill sets, you will find that the rest becomes much easier.

6. This process cannot be hurried. The knowledge you seek tends to come in its right time. Be patient. Be relaxed. Allow, rather than force, your ideas to emerge, change, form, dissolve and reform. You'll get information that may ultimately shift, and you'll draw conclusions that may ultimately shift. You'll make choices which you will reevaluate, and ultimately reevaluate again. You'll have moments of clarity which will present themselves, and then dissipate or deepen. Stay open, and notice what happens. It is a journey and it is a process: you are along for the ride. Put a special witness on your shoulder to watch the drama unfold.

7. Allow for emotion to flow. If tears or anger surface, allow them. They open doors to deeper wisdom. It's all OK.

8. You will find a list of common pitfalls following each set of questions. Please understand that these pitfalls may apply to any stage of your journey. Through 25 years of experience helping people with this kind of inquiry, I name these pitfalls for your guidance. Refer to them frequently, and make sure you are not inadvertently sabotaging your best efforts.

And so, let's delve right in with the first two questions in the series: **"What do I love?," and "What am I good at?"**

CHAPTER 11

✤

What Do I Love?
and
What Am I Good At?

"Let the beauty of what you love be what you do."
—Rumi

CONSIDERING WHAT YOU LOVE IS A GREAT PLACE TO START!
What you love and what you are naturally good at are very closely related.
There are two sets of questions in this section: the opening set focuses on
what you love; the closing set draws out your natural strengths. Feel free to
start in either place.

WHAT DO I LOVE?

- When I look at my life, work and volunteer realms, what activities most excite me and call forth my passion?

- What do I most love to do? With myself? With and for others?

- What makes me smile when I am doing or thinking about it?

- What do I read about, think about, study about, watch TV about?

- What would I love to do in this world if there were no constraints?

- Who am I, really?

- What, in the doing of it, gives me most joy and satisfaction?

- What is really the truth about me and what I love to do?

- What have I always dreamed about doing (even though I may have put it aside)?

- On what occasions in my life have I said: "I get to do this—and they pay me for it!"

Common pitfalls—in no particular order

- **"I don't deserve to name, or acknowledge, or pursue that which makes me happy."**
  This is simply a belief you adopted somewhere in the past. Perhaps the parental models in your life felt they themselves didn't have the luxury to do what they loved, but had to work hard at what paid the bills. Although those two ideas—working at what you love and being able to pay the bills—are not mutually exclusive, too often they are seen that way. For now, do your best to remove the "I don't deserve" label from anything that may appear in the answers that come to you.

- **"What I love will look 'weird' to my family and friends."**
  Here's where you'll want to exercise some courage and name what you love. Search out like-minded others to whom you can speak. I will never forget my serendipitous encounter with a woman whose passion was performing autopsies. She had been a fan of the TV show, "Quincy," and her obsession with forensic science radiated in our conversation. For now, she held a weekend post in the local Medical Examiner's office, while she waited for a full-time position.

I believe there is a place for everyone to do what they love most and do best. As you finish this process and this book, I hope you will be able to entertain—or agree with—that notion. In the meantime, keep asking and answering that first question over and over again.

- **"My answers aren't any good."**
  The self-censor tends to be ever present. Sometimes it operates below our awareness, and blocks a personal truth from even seeing the light of day. It judges ideas automatically, albeit prematurely, relying on old and internalized messages from our parents or communities.

  I believe that any answer that rings true for you can play a prominent role in your life. With a supportive team, you can find a way to make anything happen. There are, after all, people who have no educational degrees teaching in classrooms. There are people who can't sing working joyfully at the Metropolitan Opera. There are people who love to ski, and are getting paid to do exactly that, all over the world. And there are high school students leading recycling campaigns (or projects, or centers...) for their towns. My advice for this initial round is to allow your deepest self to speak. Listen to it and write down what you hear yourself say. Period.

- **"I can't ask for help."**
  We are so embedded in our habits and patterns that sometimes it is hard to think beyond them.

  An objective perspective from a coach or helper during this initial phase of inquiry may help you park your fears and identify any blocks to fully and freely answering the questions. Remember: your only assignment for now is to give voice to your thoughts and feelings. You have permission to dream and to listen to your heart's desire. If you need help doing that, ask for it.

WHAT AM I GOOD AT?

- What am I already doing and being that is working in my life?

- What do I seem to be really good at, and wonder why others can't seem to do it as well or as easily as I do?

- What am I doing when am I at my best and feel most satisfied and fulfilled? (Consider arenas of work, volunteerism, play, school, family.)

- What skills have I gained along the way that I particularly enjoy using?

- What was my favorite course in school? Where did I get good grades effortlessly?

- What do others seem to always appreciate about the way I am? Or, what I offer to the situation?

- What do I do easily and notice that for others, it is difficult?

- What am I good at that no one ever taught me?

- What is the strength or gift I find ways to use no matter in what situation in I find myself?

- Where have I exhibited competence and confidence since childhood? (Answer this yourself, and then ask parents or relatives for their reflections.)

Common pitfalls—in no particular order

- **"What I do easily and effortlessly has no commercial value."** Unexamined, this belief can stop you cold. We tend to take for granted the things we do easily, and assume anyone else can do them easily as well. The other side of that is to assume that what has value are only the skills you have had to struggle to master.

  Actually, the opposite is true. What you do easily and well is what sustains you in work. It is the difference between people who perform their job as "artists," always looking for innovative solutions, and those who simply do the motions of the job. Start noticing what you tend to contribute in every situation in which you find yourself. Start valuing what you notice as talents and gifts which are natural to you. Again, ask others. They know.

- **"I don't have a name for my unique skill."**
I encountered this myself early in my career when I was trying to do a similar exercise. My point is, notice what you do, and describe it the best that you can with as many words as you need. Your "strength" or your "passion" at this point doesn't have to conform with the list of skills in any career planning advice book. It will find its right name in time, or many names and many applications.

Don't put your life on hold until you can come up with a shiny, professional name for your unique skill. Pick a phrase that works—and tweak it as you go.

Early on, I discovered that I was good at "kicking people in the pants." In the family, in the boardroom, and with clients, I was the one who dared to ask the tough questions, and to invite active solutions.

At the time, I couldn't figure out a good name for this particular capability. So, as a joke, I made a business card illustrated with a hiking boot, a ballet shoe and a tennis sneaker. The text read: **Kick in the Pants Counseling Service: We fit the shoe to you.**

Across the next 30 years, I have come up with several names for this capability—the most recent being "Why Not Do What You Love?"

- **"I doubt that I can..." or "I'm afraid this would..."**
Sometimes we don't name what we do best because we don't dare to announce it, or because we don't want to brag, or because we think we can't do anything with it. Doubts and fears are often the first to arrive when unique and special personal qualities are first named.

While the doubts appear to be serious objections, recognize that they are just a form of your current beliefs, and very common ones at this initial stage. They have only the power you give them. Try making a list of doubts and fears as they arise—acknowledge them, respect them... and continue to move forward with your search. Consider them constructions of your mind.

- **"I just don't know how to..."**
Sometimes you may come up with a "blank." Or none of your answers grab you or feel just right. That's OK: don't let "not knowing" discourage you.

You may wish to give the following instructions to your Self on a daily basis: "I am now willing to know what I love, what makes me happy, and what gifts are mine."

If your ideas are not flowing or your clarity is blocked, stepping back and setting an intention to know what you love is a fine way to get your process back in motion. After all, you are the only one who really knows what you want. The answers are in there somewhere, and it's your job to coax them out safely and gently. If your stomach knots a little when you use the prompting phrase above, don't worry: that's a definite sign that you are right on target.

CHAPTER 12

What Do I Want?

"Many men go fishing all of their lives without knowing that it is not fish they are after."
—*Henry David Thoreau*

WHAT WE WANT—FOR OURSELVES AND FOR OTHERS—is not something that should be denied. At the least, we need to consider it freely and fully. In responding to the questions below, allow the answers to come from deep within, from needs you haven't dared name or haven't dared ask to be fulfilled. They are there. What you want is part of you, and it needs to be honored and considered.

Within this category of questions framed as "wants," you may find a lens that allows you to surface some different clues about your longings—things you have always wanted but not dared to admit to yourself, or things you were told you shouldn't have, couldn't have, or didn't deserve to have.

It's important to name your wants, every single one of them, without embarrassment. And, allow your answers to enrich your picture of who you are and what you are about.

Enjoy!

WHAT DO I WANT?

- What do I really want for my life? (Consider all realms.)

- What do I want for my home?

- What do I want for my family?

- What do I want for my health?

- What do I want for my spiritual life?

- What do I want for my financial life?

- What do I want for my professional and work life?

- What do I want for my relationships?

- What do I want for my community?

- What do I want for my legacy?

- What is the contribution I want to make to the planet?

Common pitfalls—in no particular order:

- **Thinking too small.**
  Sometimes our own censoring of big, scary, new ideas brings us down to what we know how to get, rather than what we really WANT to have or do. We are afraid, we don't know how, so we adjust our dreams downward.

  This is another tendency to notice and to temporarily park. There is energetic support for the dreams that emerge when body, mind, and spirit are aligned. Metaphorically, imagine the world like an ocean which you can petition for water. Do you bring a teaspoon...or a bathtub? The ocean won't run out of water, no matter how large a container you bring to fill.

- **Thinking you don't know.**
  All too often, we let knowledge—or more accurately, the apparent lack of knowledge of what to do—stop us from taking our next steps in life.

Actually, in some deep recess of your being, you *do* know; you are just not ready to tell yourself yet, or you don't believe you deserve to have what you want. In reality, you are the only one who does know. It's OK to stay with not-knowing for a while. It is truly a huge act of courage to sit without answers. I would suggest you also play with some positive instructions, to help unblock your willingness to know—even if you find they are uncomfortable to speak out loud:

— *I am willing to know what I want.*
— *I do deserve to articulate what I want so I can entertain it.*
— *I do deserve to actually have what I want.*

- **Overfocusing on what you don't want.**
  Unfortunately, too much attention to what we don't want tends to draw that very aspect into our lives. For example, repeatedly thinking I don't want to struggle with money continuously creates the image of struggling with money. Too much attention to how hard your dream might be to achieve also creates the image of struggle.

  Pay attention to the ways you phrase your desires. This is about what you *do* want—*I want, do, have, be* _____ *in a way that's easy.* In contrast, consider this phrase: *I want to have financial freedom and money flowing into my life effortlessly.* And be sure to picture it in living color and all its glory.

- **Confusing the "what" with the "how."**
  When you involve yourself in contemplating WHETHER you can do it, or HOW you can do it, you start on an unnecessary detour that tends to block creative thinking about what you really DO want.

  Asking the "how" question comes at a later stage in this process. Right now you are concerned with the "what" of your life, the DESIRED OUTCOME or the IDEAL RESULT.

Suspend any need to know the "hows." Many "hows" will emerge, some of which will create themselves out of the synchronicity and mystery that accompany deep intention and surrender.

- **Focusing on the desire/need for money.**
  Money is one of the "hows" that can become a big distraction if you let it become your primary goal. Consider what you want the money for. That is closer to the real want.

Many business networking classes feature a practice that has come to be known as "the elevator talk." In fact, one day while channel surfing, I saw an elevator talk competition featured on a business channel. Assuming that folks with great ideas only get a few minutes to grab another's attention, young aspiring entrepreneurs were trained to hone their ideas of what they want to do, practice them, and actually present them to real venture capitalists in a two-minute elevator ride. If their idea was compelling, inspiring, and good for people and the planet, the funders *gave them money*, along with a critique and good ideas.

It is the ideas and your clarity about your ideas that attract solutions, in whatever form—money included. If you want money to buy an organic farm, focus on the farm you want to have and on the life you envision there, and see what happens. Money is one of the ways to get there and it is not the only way. We just don't know how things are going to come to us.

- **Confusing intention with expectation.**
  Putting out an intention is different from having an expectation. The two are important to distinguish, as one serves you more than the other. Your intention is a way of being. An expectation is generally attached to how or when a specific outcome might manifest. The example that comes to mind is the labyrinth (ancient configuration for a walking meditation) that my housemate and I conceived and intended for the meadow behind the house. Had we had an expectation, and a big plan, for how and when it would be constructed, we would have missed the miracles that started

to unfold when we started talking about our intention and desired out-come with others. The wood chips were gifted and delivered in abundance. Someone contributed a bench made out of a fallen tree. Needed bricks hiding on a corner of the property were spotted. A neighbor knew where to get rope for marking the path. Actually, it was a life-changing event to watch this labyrinth, which apparently wanted to come to life, manifest in three weeks. I hesitate to think how any expectations of how this should have proceeded might have interfered with the mysterious natural process.

Responding to the questions in this Chapter may lead you to thoughts about what you might want for your family, your community, or the planet... which leads to the topic of Contribution. When you are ready, lean into the next Chapter with all your intentions for a better world for all of us.

CHAPTER 13

What Do I Want for the World?

"Shaping the world we want takes audacity and persistence."
—Joanne Reich

IN A WORLD THAT'S HUNGRY FOR YOUR TALENTS, what you love to do becomes a unique and welcomed contribution. In fact, I will repeat what I stated earlier: **You may be starving for lack of an opportunity to give your best gifts.** This could be a win-win.

What do I want for the world? I'm taking author's prerogative to start with my personal list. I hope it will encourage you to list your deepest desires, dreams and wants for the world in which we live. If you find yourself noticing what my list omits, let it be a signal to you about what you care about. Put that item on your list.

As I write this during 2009, I look forward to the administration of a new president and share the high hopes and new energy that seem to be swirling around him and the changes he has promised.

At the moment of this writing, we have suffered a financial crisis, looked an energy and global warming crisis straight in the eye, and suffered the loss of a half million jobs per month. All of this exacerbates crises in education, health care, Medicare and Social Security. Whether or not you see these things as current crises, emerging crises, or simply big problems needing to be faced, I leave you to select your label. However, I think we all began to agree by December of 2008 that we're in this together and we've got some work to do.

- I wish for everyone the privilege and pleasure of knowing what they love and do well, and being able to create opportunities to do more of it.

- I'd like to see us all individually fit, active, and taking responsibility for our own health and well-being.

- I'd like to see everyone with access to health care, with emphasis on prevention and healthy eating.

- I'd like to see us growing food in our gardens, or making community gardens, and cooking the produce in our homes.

- I'd like to see fast-food establishments shifting their role to promoting health and their clientele demanding it of them.

- I'd like to see food corporations using natural sweeteners and avoiding the addictive empty calories of white sugar and white flour in their products.

- I'd like all citizens to have free access to information about natural health remedies without interference.

- I'd like the television stations to be free of direct consumer drug advertising, as is the practice in Europe.

- I'd like mainstream medicine to be open to—and honor—the complementary approaches to health which cost less and are often more effective—even in serious cases.

- I really want clean air and clean water as rights of life for all humankind.

- I'd like individuals and communities to consider zero waste as a goal, as some cities are starting to do.

- I'd like each child to have attentive, skilled parents and other adult advocates and teachers in their lives.

- I'd like to see our schools as small communities, where every child is seen, known and cared for.

- I'd like to see parenting be an unapologetically joyful and recognized calling.

- I'd like schools to be headed by strong leader principals who have the skill and talent to mobilize teachers and students to high standards of character, creative achievement, emotional health, and community involvement.

- I'd like our communities to be more friendly to walkers and bikers, with land use plans that serve present needs without compromising the needs of the future.

- I'd like individuals to buy cars that use less gas, and car corporations to make them for us, using their advertising dollars to promote them for us.

- I'd like our government to do appropriate monitoring on our behalf such that misplaced incentives in our financial regulatory systems can be caught early and righted.

- I'd like organizations dealing in any aspect of finance for consumers to have the highest ethical standards and pay attention to basics—as does my community bank, which is still solvent and healthy.

- I'd like young people to be equipped to manage their money at an early age and to adopt habits to save for their futures.

NOW IT'S YOUR TURN TO MAKE A LIST:

Ask yourself: "What do I want for the world?"

Use your journal, or a yellow pad.

Take as many pages as you want.

Keep a running list.

Watch how your ideas emerge, develop, shift, deepen.

Common pitfalls—in no particular order

- **"I have to do it all myself."**
  Sometime we discount an idea immediately because we think we can't do it ourselves. Don't sell yourself short. Be willing to just plant seeds for your idea. Remember: at this point, we are gaining clarity, not taking action. Stay with the process. Don't let your fears and worries about being inadequate for the task derail you. The world is full of helpers whom we haven't yet met, in case you decide to pursue a particular "want" more actively.

- **"I can't do what I want unless other people change..."**
  This question is about how you want things to be, in your world, in your community, in your family, without expectation that anyone else will change. It is not about insinuating how your spouse should change, nor demanding what the president should do, nor waiting around for some other organization or person to take action.

Your vision has power. It suggests how you might contribute by starting with yourself. Think about 2006 Nobel Prize winner Muhammad Yunus (**muhammadyunus.org**). He made a big difference in a large part of the Third World because he envisioned that poor rural women had the power to improve their lives if given access to credit and peer support.

So, *he* changed the way *he* did business. Already a banker, *he* established the Grameen Bank to provide seed capital in the form of micro-credit loans, which garnered a return on investment from 95% of the borrowers. Now known as "banker to the poor," his model worked so well to build self-confidence, stabilize families, improve nutrition and offer access to education for rural families that it has spread across the globe and garnered him a Nobel Peace Prize.

What you want for the world is a small step into the next question, "How do I wish to serve?" If the perceived needs around you are occupying your attentions and your energies, perhaps you'd like to apply your gifts to a particular issue and do something that only you can do, on a scale that you can manage. Hold on to that thought as we continue to use the final questions to help us gather more information about ourselves.

CHAPTER 14

❧

How Do I Wish to Serve?

"Everything I did in my life that was worthwhile I caught hell for."
—*Chief Justice Earl Warren*

THE FINAL QUESTIONS IN THE SERIES INVITE YOU to connect with the causes that motivate you to serve. The notion of "making a difference" is something that is both appealing and healing. I have always wanted to know that my life mattered, and as I talk to my peers, this is a frequent part of our conversation.

On the one hand, the notion of how to make a difference is simple. According to Mother Theresa, you can "find someone who thinks she is alone and let her know she is not."

On the other hand, the notion of making a difference can be intimidating. When I think of someone like one of my local heroes, David Mazor, who provided a million books to devastated school libraries after Hurricane Katrina, I start questioning myself. "What can I do?" And then I remember that David Mazor is an ordinary man who simply started out by wanting books to have more than one life—to serve a variety of purposes. When he realized how many good books were being thrown into landfills or were languishing in retired professors' basements, he started collecting them to distribute to impoverished libraries and school districts across the US.

When I first heard about David's project, I delivered boxes of books from my personal library to his garage, relieved that they might have a new home. His newsletter, Reader-to-Reader, has since shown me how his initial, simple efforts earned him storage space at Amherst College. There is also a growing exchange between book recipients on Indian reservations and Amherst College student tutors. The project has taken on a life of its own and keeps growing, including the donations to New Orleans.

When I feel intimidated by people who have performed what I consider to be great service, I have to remember that personal passion magnetizes energy and funding and ideas. You start where you are. You give what you have. You keep going. The oft-repeated starfish story inspires me every time I come across it.

ONCE A MAN WAS WALKING ALONG A BEACH. The sun was shining and it was a beautiful day. Off in the distance, he could see a person going back and forth between the surf's edge and the beach. Back and forth this person went. As the man approached he could see that there were hundreds of starfish stranded on the sand as the result of the natural action of the tide.

The man was struck by the apparent futility of the task. There were far too many starfish. Many of them were sure to perish. As he approached, the person continued the task of picking up starfish one by one and throwing them into the surf.

He said, "You must be crazy. There are thousands of miles of beach covered with starfish. You can't possibly make a difference." The person looked at the man. He then stooped down and picked up one more starfish and threw it back into the ocean. He smiled back at his interrogator and said: "It sure made a difference to that one."

If the economic collapse is a wake-up call for you, or if you are moved by a sense that some fundamentals in our society are due for a restructuring, maybe this is the time for a deeper look at yourself. How can you serve with joy and pride, using your very gifts, interests and obsessions to address some of our world's most pressing problems?

Clearly, there is a range of opportunity to contribute to economic, social and environmental justice—along with sustainability for this planet. You start somewhere and follow the flow. Neither Muhammad Yunus nor Martin Luther King had any idea they would be the people with the gifts and skills that a moment in history would require—or that both would receive a Nobel Peace Prize for their world-changing efforts.

Nor did David Mazor realize that his passion to recycle books intended for dumpsters to less well-endowed libraries and classrooms in our country would result in the mentoring of Indian reservation students by young people attending Amherst College. Or that his newsletter would inspire a flood of donations: two million books as of this writing. David's mission is powerful, given the fact that 60% of underprivileged children do not own a single book, which means, as he points out on his website, that a well-stocked school library in an impoverished school is a critical resource—a necessity, not a luxury. David and his team at Reader-to-Reader are out "to change the world, one book at a time." **Visit www.readertoreader.org.**

We do not always know where we will be called. However, we can begin by knowing what calls us.

Questions may illuminate your higher calling or, if you prefer, your deeper calling, or your soul's purpose. And that is what these final questions are designed to help you decipher.

HOW DO I WISH TO SERVE?

- What would my community/neighborhood look like when it is operating at its best?

- And what role do I feel called to play in that scenario?

- What would my organization look like when it is operating at its best?

- And what role might I take in that system?

- What would my world look like when it is operating at its best?

- And what might be my role in that?

- Where have I noticed unnecessary waste that I could do something about?

- Of the needs around me, which most attract my attention?

- Where have I been "called" to volunteer or offer my services in a way that has fulfilled me?

- In what ways do I personally wish to stop colluding with the continuation of the problems I see around me?

- What is my grand vision for my life and work in the world?

- If my passion were to tackle a small piece of that grand vision, what would that piece be?

- How have I noticed, as I look over my life, the ways I seem to have been living out a purpose? What do I tend to contribute or like to contribute no matter where I am?

And, finally, two questions you've probably seen before:

- When I reach my deathbed, what is it about my life I'd most like to be proud of?

- What would I like to have said in my obituary?

Much of this book was written in the months surrounding our new president's Inauguration and his repeated calls for volunteerism. On the Sunday following the Inauguration, the minister of our small New England interfaith community invited us to share what our group of older, generally liberal, white women were feeling. What resonated with me were the expressions among the gathered group of a lifting of cynicism, a deepening of relief and a new hope for the future.

One woman told about her sister, an apolitical suburban Mom for most of her life, who was now, for the very first time, researching recycling. She was planning to get involved in her town's efforts to be more responsible and sustainable. This woman quoted her sister as saying: "After this election, I am finally free to care about what happens in my world. I finally think that something I could do might make a difference."

I found her remarks so moving that I want to highlight the questions behind them. Perhaps you, too, are now freer to care and to cherish. We have been given permission, and we have been asked to help, no matter our political affiliation.

Two more powerful questions:

- What am I finally free to care about in the world?

- In what areas, and to whom, do I wish to extend more "caring"?

Common pitfalls—in no particular order:

- **Be aware of wanting to serve in order to "fix" yourself.**
  Desires that are based in "wanting to be a better person" tend to have a subtext: "I am only OK if I'm doing something for others." This underlying belief works against your natural talents, and the "doing for others" efforts can be inappropriately tainted by your other agenda for yourself.

  Let your desires to serve be a natural outgrowth of your passions, your skills, and your interests—as well as your wounds. Seek a venue that needs you as much as you need to be there. A joyful win-win.

- **Be aware of wanting to be too helpful.**
  Wanting to "help" is a natural inclination. Wanting to "help" too much carries a subtext about the helplessness of the other person. It can be perceived as judgmental. As author Peter Block said: "Stop being helpful and just get interested."

And now we take a deliberate pause for reflection on all the information that you have gathered about yourself.

Reflection

You've come to the place where you have been probing yourself, asking lots of questions, and doing your best to tll your truth to yourself.

— Get a cup or tea or coffee, find a quiet spot, sit down.

— Appreciate that there is nothing to do right now.

— Take a long, low, deep breath.

What is the truth that is emerging for you?

And, most important...

What's becoming clear to you?

PART THREE

Take Time to Pause
and Reflect

TAKE TIME TO PAUSE AND REFLECT

HERE WE ARE AT PART THREE. It is a temporary stopping place where there are no chapters to peruse and nothing much to do, except to listen to yourself. I'm calling it a pause—for reflection.

Some of you will find yourself skilled at "pausing," stopping, emptying yourself, getting a cup of tea and looking out the window. If you are one of those, you already know how the pause refreshes. You already relish how being still allows your thoughts to drift and wander, how your deepest wisdom has the space and permission to come forth. After all, in this pausing space, there is nowhere to go and nothing to do—at least for as long a time as you allow yourself.

What is becoming clear to me?

Who knows what will have become clear to you from Part One and Part Two? With your deliberations to date, perhaps you are aware that you know exactly what to do next and have no need for a pause or a reflection or, for that matter, the rest of the book. Or, perhaps you are aware you have come to a fork in the road and some tough decisions will be required. Or perhaps you need to just sit for a while with what you've unearthed so far, and let it percolate and gestate for days or weeks until your deeper wisdom offers up some next steps.

For example: A friend, using the process in the book, identified her special skill of listening deeply and gently supporting the emergence of people's voices. In her moment of pausing, what came to her was the realization about why she had been so disoriented when her children went off to college. Her special gift, applied joyfully to parenting, was no longer in demand on a 24/7 basis. The question emerged, "In what other venue could I express that gift?"

For those of you who know how to "pause," I leave you here to enjoy your time with our central question: "What is becoming clear to me?"

For those readers who are approaching this task of finding your calling and contribution with some urgency, I offer you these additional thoughts about pausing. Perhaps you, like me for most of my life, never really mastered the ability to stop what you are doing and pause. If "doing you" means that you are in perpetual motion, working your goals and staying on task, I strongly urge you to find a way to help yourself take a break. A break opens space for something new, perhaps unexpected, and quite often useful.

In my early professional life, I took pauses in the form of short vacations, when I was so tired there was no other option. I forced myself to stop. My assistant remembers "pouring" me onto the plane to lie on the beach at Club Med for a week. Coming from a thrifty New England family, splurging on myself and doing "nothing" was not comfortable. I generally believed that I was not worthy of the "self-indulgence" of simply enjoying the ocean.

At that time, I was really a novice at pausing. I am embarrassed to disclose that I brought work with me on that trip. However small that step of taking time for a break may have been, it was a step that made me proud. I'd had the courage to at least "start" breaking the pattern of never giving myself a break. It was then I discovered philosopher monk Thomas Merton's short poem, *Nothing Doing*, which reappears from my files whenever I need it.

"Some of us need to discover that we will not begin to live more fully until we have the courage to do and see and taste and experience much less than usual."

— THOMAS MERTON—

What I do remember about those forced pauses is how refreshed I felt afterwards. I felt clear, relaxed, and reenergized. My path forward would often alter creatively after I had allowed myself serious time to pause.

Although I've gotten better at pausing, I'm far from having gained mastery. Having recently fallen and broken my arm, I was confined to a hospital bed for two weeks and homebound for three more. This time to "do nothing" and be totally taken care of was actually a gift that I didn't know I needed.

Given my modus operandi of simply keeping going, I had not realized that even "retired" people have to stop. We who already see ourselves as doing "much less than usual" still need the refreshment of doing—actually—nothing. After my deep rest, I noted that the ability to reflect came in its own time. With the gift of time for thought, I found myself gratefully shifting and deepening my approach to this book. And I renewed my vow to more consciously pause and rest in the future.

As you take your break, be patient with yourself. The importance of real pauses, and of doing not much of anything, is underrated. Trust that the ideas you've been working on are still working within you, even though you are not consciously thinking about them.

As you become ready, you'll start feeling your answers to the following central question emerge, and you can more actively track those answers.

WHAT IS BECOMING CLEAR TO ME?

When you are ready, you may find it helpful to journal, to keep track of your emerging insights. Writing down your thoughts—following a trail of a thought with your pen—is a generative act. It often helps you see something or know something that you hadn't seen or known before.

Here are some more active ways to enter the reflective space of the pause that refreshes:

- If, like me, words like amble, languish, linger, ponder, wander aimlessly, meander, or soften have been part of neither your vocabulary nor your behavioral repertoire, you can start by putting them on your "to do" list for 30 minutes on any given day. What I have discovered is that by just saying those words and contemplating their meaning, the ability to relax, even for a moment, emerges. You deserve time to "linger" and to "savor" your reflections.

- Nourish the pieces of the dreams you have. Hold them in your mind. Envision them. Keep them close. See them as possible. Write them down. **And/or**

- Each day, notice 3 joys—places, people, circumstances, activities, experiences, situations, service—in which you felt pleasure...however momentary it may have been. Write them down. **And/or**

- Find a quiet time and space each day where you can sit with your commitment—and repeat it out loud: *I am willing to receive information about the gifts I am meant to use at this time in my life.* **And/or**

- Review your previous work and select the questions that most resonated with you for whatever reason. Note which of the questions called forth answers that gave you joy, or elicited the response—*If only I could!* **And/or**

- What are the larger questions that may need to be addressed?
  —"What are the questions I am really struggling with?"
  —"What price am I willing to pay in order to live my personal truth?"

If you choose, you can also use this break to do some exploring in the world outside yourself.

- Talk to one person a week, or find one illustration from a book or newspaper or TV about someone doing what they love and serving others at the same time. See what resonates for you. These examples are truly EVERYWHERE. **And/or**

- Find someone that is actually engaged in what you would like to do and ask them for a conversation or interview. Prepare your questions ahead of time, and thank them for their time.

- Talk to members of your family about your dreams. Let them know about your desire to meet your own needs for financial stability and right work, and your wish to cooperate with theirs, as well.

In other words, while you may put down the book in order to pause and reflect, don't forget the reason you picked it up in the first place. Honor your need and desire to express and share your gifts in the world. Keep reflecting and realizing how you are special and unique. When you are ready to do more about it, help will appear.

There is only one common rule in finding the special truth valid for you. That is to learn to listen patiently into yourself, to give yourself a chance to find your own way which is yours and nobody else's way... .

The basic truth in the teachings of all mankind amount to only one common thing: To find your way to the thing you feel when you love dearly, or when you create, or when you build your home, or when you give birth to your children or when you look at the stars at night.

—WILHELM REICH—

Again.... pause and reflect for as long as you wish. Create some form of relaxing daily process so that you can listen to your own truth. When you are ready to make changes, manifest your dreams, create a life experiment, or elicit even more clarity about what you want to do, you will find ways to do so as you enter Parts Four and Five.

PART FOUR

Take Time to Align Your Intentions

TAKE TIME TO ALIGN YOUR INTENTIONS

IN PART FOUR, we enter a new energetic space which I am choosing to call THE BIG NUDGE. As I have noted several times, our "calling," the life we are meant to lead, the work that is ours to do, can't be willed into us. We are born to it and we discover it, or we don't.

As we enter the "Big Nudge," we will get more directive. There are ways to pay attention to the clues we are getting about the meaning of our lives and there are ways of playing with those clues that can move us closer to what might be our calling. We can stay attentive to our possibilities in a positive and proactive way.

Sometimes the best helping hand you can get is a good, firm push.

— JOANN THOMAS —

Consider that as we go through life, there may be times when we do gain a sense about what is clearly most satisfying to us. While we feel tempted to enter that "calling" space, it's very easy to talk ourselves out of it.

- "It will never support me financially."
- "My friends will think I'm crazy."
- "I don't dare try something that has never been done the way I'd like to do it."
- "I don't dare to anger my boss (my spouse, my children, my colleagues)."
- "It will never work for me to do what I love, and have a family, too."
- "I can't do this alone."
- "I'm not good enough to tackle such a big issue."
- "I can't claim my freedom and live with the consequences."

Yes, we have loves, and passions, and callings to service; we also have reluctance, cautions, and objections. Those are the constructs that hold us back.

In Part Four, you will be invited to respond to Three Questions which represent the core of my professional work for 25 years. These Questions will take you through a powerful process of exploration and reflection. They will invite you to tell more of your own truth: What's your intention? What stops you from doing more of what you say you want to do?
And how can you transform hurdles into platforms on which to build something new?

Remember that the Three Questions are intended to allow you to:

- courageously step into the future you are beginning to craft for yourself

- surface the reasons you may be hesitating to claim your birthright, and

- clarify the choices entailed in moving forward to do more of what you love.

I urge you to keep following this process in the sequence laid out. Remember you are still in exploration, discovery, contemplation, and planning. In this process you can try out tentative and temporary decisions virtually without risk. It is helpful to remind yourself that, no matter what you decide, you never lose your ability to stop, to revisit your choices, and choose again.

So turn the page and let's get started.

CHAPTER 15

QUESTION ONE:
What's My Intention?

*"Martin Luther King famously proclaimed, 'I have a dream,'
not, 'I have an issue.'"*
—*Van Jones*

IT IS MY BELIEF THAT SOMEWHERE WITHIN YOU lies your destiny, your path, and your core purpose. My hope is that as you read Parts One and Two, you were able to give yourself more permission to see what it is you are meant to be about.

You may remember the story of Michelangelo, who was once asked how he could have created something as magnificent as the statue of David. He replied that David was there all along. He, Michaelangelo, simply chiseled away everything that wasn't David, and found him there in all his glory.

My friend and colleague, Judy Grupenhoff, featured this story along with the following commentary on her website, the Power Center. **Visit www.powerctr.com.** Judy helps people align internal energies and release energetic blocks, in order to pursue their core purposes. Here's what she says:

"Each of us has a David within us—a spark of divine essence, one's true self. Everyone has had moments, however fleeting, when we have experienced the awareness, peace, and power that come from connecting with that spark. This is our natural state of being, but more often than not we find ourselves living lives full of stress and anxiety, trying to live up to others' expectations or battling the belief that we are just not good enough, not smart enough, not successful enough, not anything enough. We live life not as who we really are, but as who we have come to believe we are. Our true self may be there somewhere, but all we see is the marble."

To help uncover more of who you are, we're about to experiment with a brief, energizing description of your intentions. I'll give you some templates to help you focus and summarize your conclusions about your gifts, strengths, loves, passions, and calls to service you've already identified.

It's important to remember your description is not engraved in stone—it can be revised and refined. I invite you to be as clear and precise as you can be. How do you want to use your gifts and skills for this period of your life? The clarity with which you articulate your current intentions will attract results more quickly than you can imagine. So... What's up for you at this point? What do you really want to do next? What do you want this next part of your life to be about? Here's where you allow your special talents to be uniquely visible in the world.

WHAT'S MY INTENTION?

How to work with this question

Frame your stated intention in a way that is positive, powerful, and clear. To help you with this process, I offer two Templates below. Play with either, or both. It may take several tries, and that's ok—sometimes clarity comes on the third try...or the tenth. Above all, be sure to have fun.

Template #1: Statement of Intention

You can extend the work you have already done by completing a Statement of Intention.

Using my (special gifts of) _____, _____, _____,
I now enjoy (doing, creating, performing, building) _____,
In order to (ultimate
outcome)_____.

EXAMPLES:

Using my passion for listening, inviting forward people's voices, and reflecting their message,
I now enjoy creating promotional materials for companies...
So that behavior and messages are aligned, and thus attract more of the kind of clients they want to serve.

Here's another approach that same person might use:

Using my passion for listening, welcoming people's writing and speaking, and providing encouraging feedback,

I now lead writing and self-discovery workshops for college freshmen...
So that they have a means for discovering and honoring their unique and valuable voices.

Here's one for a different person with different gifts and desires:

Using my experience as a welfare mother, my gift of writing, my natural ability to empower others, and my passion to share useful information where it is needed,

I create highly useful community access informational videos...
So that others can learn how to both navigate within and move out of the welfare system.

Here's one for a different person with different gifts and less specific needs. You will note that they have not yet specified an activity they want to pursue. Perhaps they are not yet clear. What they do know is that they want to attract information and connections that will enable them to refine their focus.

Using my passion for "green," and my skill to fix anything mechanical,

I easily attract information about places and people where and with whom I can move forward...

In order to be of service to the planet in my local area.

You, too, can frame an intention to "attract" knowledge about what you want, whether it is customers, information, insight, new ideas, or supplies. What information or knowledge or tools would help you move forward? Again, I suggest that you not focus on money just yet. Rather, focus on what it is you want to do with the money. What would the money buy? What would it allow you to do? Focus on your true goal, and allow it to find its own way into your life.

Template #2: Statement of Intention—Affirmation

This is a simple statement of intention, framed as if it were already in place. These kinds of statements are often called "affirmations." They affirm what you are wanting, in living color, as if you already have it. Brain scientists tell us that the brain is literal in the way it receives ideas and instructions. Give it the present-focused instruction it needs to allow it to work for you.

State your intention in a positive way, and include yourself as the primary actor, moving the activity forward. Note the use of active verbs, and the emotional tone of excitement.

EXAMPLES:

- I now easily seek out and attract three classes per week, where I invite college freshmen to find their voices as writers and as human beings. My consulting practice is magnetic and profitable.

- My business is a green business. My employees and I demonstrate measurable progress in waste disposal, product safety, energy use reduction, and conservation of all kinds. We use our own work as a model, and eagerly share our progress and our discoveries about best practices.

- I'm excited about being a conscious and committed parent. I now easily and enjoyably spend three hours a day reading, talking with, or playing with my children. I set boundaries on TV viewing, so that it is a limited caretaker in our home.

- I now notice and regularly write down the activities that excite me, and I'm willing for this to be different from the plans my parents have always held for me.

- I've easily turned what I love to do for others into an all-service helping business. I cook, do errands, and give massages—and I easily spread the word about what I offer. I love to work for the people who love to have me work for them. The clients I seek are also seeking me.

If you haven't already done so, take pencil and paper and craft your statement. Use either or both templates or create one of each. Play with the words and ideas. Initial drafts may be longish. That's OK, as you are using the process to think your intention through. Once you are clear, you can easily shorten your sentence to summarize everything to which you know it refers.

Say your statement. Sing your statement. And if it feels a bit uncomfortable, read what follows before you consider changing it. Because....when you frame a powerful statement that describes what you want as if you already have it, you will have feelings. Here's some of what you might expect in no particular order:

- **A thrill in your gut, and a sense of relief.** Finally: yes, yes, yes! This is what you have wanted, and you have never articulated it before. WOW!

- **A nervous tingling in your gut.** Don't try to suppress this one. If what you've identified stretches you in some new way, or is something about which you have doubts, you will feel both a charge of excitement and a flash of fear. You are pushing your own boundaries, and that's probably a good thing to sit with for a while.

- **A flood of internal objections.** These will come up naturally. The "new you" that you are creating has caused the "old you" to become nervous. The "old you" wants the comfort of the status quo and will do anything at all to "protect" you from discomfort and from the states of confusion and not-knowing. Don't worry; it's important to recognize and honor these objections as they arise. Take note of them, as they will actually become tools for you when we come to our second question.

- **Lots of second-guessing.** "Maybe that's unrealistic, maybe I can't do that." A desire to lower the bar you've set—a bit, or a lot. Honor these, too. And don't be too quick to act to relieve the tension you may feel. When moving into new space, these reactions are entirely normal.

- **Internal combat sufficient to bring on temporary confusion** and feelings of depression. You've set up a real challenge. Your newly-crafted Statement of Intention invites your old thinking patterns for a duel. Stay in the game, at least for the short term, by focusing daily on what you say you want. This will help your new intention to survive and thrive. The tension will pass, providing you stay on track with your decision. Stay with it long enough to let your old automatic fears dissipate. Reaffirm that you've done your best in the past, and now you are inviting something new to the table.

- **You may get new information** with which to refine your initial Statement of Intention. Yes: after the internal battle of ideas has subsided, you may legitimately want to refine and calibrate your initial statement. You may discover that the leap you want to make is too big at this moment. You'll know whether you need to moderate your stated intention or gather some real-life allies to help you address the apparent intimidation or hurdles.

It takes courage to stay with this process. Being temporarily confused and fearful about what's ahead during a process of change is common and normal. Patience needs a strong invitation to the party, and professional helpers may be useful. A coach can certainly provide perspective when you are inaugurating important changes for yourself.

What's next?

Play with your Statement of Intention. Repeat it several times a day. Talk about it in the most positive ways—primarily to yourself. *"This is what I want to do, or do more of….and this is what my life looks like when I'm doing it."* Allow more ideas to come and, if they enrich your vision, enlarge it, or make it more potent or more fun, add them to the statement. Don't worry about the "how"—we're still on the "what."

In other words, get your mind used to this new construct, and let your new intention take up more space in your mind's eye than the objections and fears that may surround it. Liken it to practicing a new tennis stroke or golf swing, which feels quite uncomfortable and even distasteful at first until you get used to it. Without practice, your body will never swing the racket or club in a new way. It works the same with your mind when your habits of thinking meet new possibilities. Practice regularly with your new ideas, no matter the initial discomfort.

And now let's face Question Two and explore any sources of discomfort or tension you may be feeling about what you have just laid out for yourself.

CHAPTER 16

QUESTION TWO:

Why Might I be Unwilling to Do What I Say I Want?

*"Each of us guards a gate of change
that can only be opened from the inside…"*
—*Marilyn Ferguson*

YOU JUST CREATED AND WROTE DOWN your Statement of Intention that answers Question One. Now it is time to make sure that all parts of you are aligned with that intention and moving in the same direction.

"Why might 'unwillingness' be such an issue?" you ask. After all, you've just spent hours crafting and writing down your intentions! Question Two seems to more than insinuate a serious self-imposed block on your part. Don't be offended: let me explain.

As I said earlier, most psychologists agree that we humans are always doing what we perceive to be in our best interests. When we resist advice, or even when we resist our own positive intentions, there is generally good reason. We simply don't always know what that reason is. We may not be aware of the undercurrents of wisdom, fear, or needs that drive our hesitation to step out into "the new." If you continue to say you want something different than what you have, and you do nothing about it, you at least owe yourself an inquiry into what may be holding you back. Consider the wisdom and insights that will result from your inquiry as the gifts of this chapter.

One element of maturity is the ability to take deep responsibility for every aspect of our lives—including unconscious habits, beliefs and desires. "Taking deep responsibility" means we acknowledge that whatever we are doing or not doing in this life is our choice—at some level. That bears repeating:

"Taking deep responsibility" means we acknowledge that whatever we are doing or not doing in this life is our choice—at some level. It's quite freeing to take that responsibility. Being responsible for the results we get in life puts us entirely in charge. We can change what we are doing or not doing and get some different results!

Question Two gives you the opportunity to tell your own truth about what's going on. This question invites you to be more clear with yourself about your willingness to actually manifest what you want. Are there doubts and fears negating, sabotaging or energetically blocking the full spirit of your intention?

This is not gratuitous mucking around in the psyche. Imagine that you seek to go somewhere, and one leg takes off in one direction and the other in the opposite. You wouldn't get very far very fast. Conflicting energies hold you back in the same way. Your intention is going in one direction; your fear leads you in another, albeit unconsciously. You need to get acquainted with your conflicting energies. They are not blameworthy—they just are. Once you access your own truth about the matter, the conflict is usually address-able, given your deep commitment to do more of what you love in your life.

It is always worth a check—a "willingness check," if you will—to make sure all of your energies are engaged in pursuing the Intentions that you lay out for yourself. If you are like most people who are formulating bold new plans, you have already noticed some fears and doubts. Becoming more aware of your objections is sort of like preparing for company: you pick up and put away the children's toys in the living room, which you have always detoured around, but which might trip up an unsuspecting guest.

Here's a true example of how this willingness check works.

Susan was an insurance broker. She loved her business, and loved providing her clients with peace of mind. She was personable, competent, disciplined and enthusiastic. And she wanted to attract and serve more clients.

When Susan probed herself with the question: "Why might I be

122

unwilling?" she was surprised to find that one of the answers was, "It isn't OK for me to earn more money than my father did." Some would call that an energetic script; others would label it an "old belief needing to be updated." Whatever the label, it sets up a conflict. Susan had determined at an earlier time in her life that outpacing her father financially would dismiss his accomplishments in some way. That early conclusion operated as a very effective saboteur of her own efforts to grow.

Being willing to discover, take responsibility for, and "own" conclusions you have made under earlier circumstances means you can also update them. Although astonished at the content of her inner objection, Susan also recognized the truth of it. She decided it would be true no longer. She realized that she could be loyal and respectful to her father by being as successful as he would have wanted her to be.

With that refreshed conclusion, Susan broke through her self-imposed ceiling, her "unwillingness." She no longer needed to cap her desire to provide peace of mind to a larger number of people through customized insurance products. Her business started growing immediately.

Susan's is just one example of unwillingness. As long as her old belief remained operative in some corner of her mind, it blocked her sincere intentions to build a larger practice. Fortunately, she was able to transform the identified unwillingness into a new way of looking at her situation. She was free to achieve as much as she wished. You can do the same.

By discovering and neutralizing your internal blocks and updating them for your present circumstances, your willingness will be free to expand. You will discover that it is suddenly much easier to bring your Intentions to life and achieve your goals. Unwillingness, in whatever form it may take, is yours to acknowledge, neutralize, update, and release, so that all of your energy is ready to move forward in the direction you intend.

So, here we go...

WHY MIGHT I BE UNWILLING?

How to work with this question

This question requires dedicating some time and sitting down, whether it be under a tree in the park, or in a part of your home where you will not be disturbed. Before you start, be sure to gather a pen or pencil, and a pad of lined paper. For this process, I strongly encourage you to follow the steps below in sequence.

1. Make sure your statement of intent is articulated with brevity, confidence and power. If it isn't, rework it until it is.

2. When it is, write it down at the top of the page.

3. Ask yourself "Why might I be unwilling to do, be, or have _____?" Number and record your answers in the order in which they come to your mind, without censorship. If you have a friend or a coach, that person can repeatedly ask you the question and record your answers so you are completely free to respond spontaneously.

4. Keep repeating the question. You will know you've hit paydirt when you feel a charge of connection in your body. Sometimes that happens at answer number five, or number 12, or number 26. Sometimes it doesn't even come on the first day. You may need to let the challenge of this question percolate within you for a while.

5. Notice that some of what comes up may be embarrassing to admit, but stay with it: there very well may be a crucial nugget of wisdom hidden there. Whatever it is, it is. And you need to know about it.

6. You may need a clear-minded helper to assist you to allow and accept difficult answers, whatever they are. Invite your unconscious to offer words or images, and welcome whatever comes, including the surprises. Those often provide the biggest payoff.

7. Keep probing with new ways to ask the same question. Go deeper. If your answer on the initial round is: "I don't know..." ask again: Why might I be unwilling to know what is holding me back?

- Why might I be unwilling to move ahead on what I have said I wanted to do in my life?

- Why might I be unwilling to take a stand in my workplace for more "green" practices?

- Why might I be unwilling to seek training for the professional certification I've always wanted to have?

- Why might I be unwilling to experiment on a part-time basis with this new idea I have?

8. Sometimes it helps to probe by completing the sentences below:

I might be afraid that...
I might not deserve that...
I might not be capable of...
I might not know how to...
I might not be safe if...

9. Sometimes the probing can take a different tack:

I'm concerned my father/mother would think...
I'm concerned my spouse/partner would think...
I'm concerned my boss/colleagues would think...
The fear that holds me back is...

The bottom line, here, is something that I've said before: People most often do what they perceive to be in their best interest. That means you can assume that, at some level, you have a very logical reason for doing or not doing what you intend for yourself.

Remember the earlier example of Susan, who feared that if she grew her business according to her goals, she would be dishonoring the memory of her father. Performing a "willingness check" allows you to ferret out hidden reasons for your hesitancy to move forward. Once you have these nuggets, new wisdom and new perspectives will emerge, and you will be freer and more able to move forward with your Calling.

Common pitfalls—in no particular order

- **Censuring serendipitous answers that don't fit with your view of yourself.**
  The actual "truth" of your reluctance is often embarrassing to admit. You can count on it. (Look back at the example of Susan.)

  Allow and invite any embarrassment that accompanies your inquiry. It is what it is. Delight that you have found a key puzzle piece to unlocking your own possibilities. Although the idea of your believing x, y, or z may be unwelcome, you can deliberately rejoice that you've found something very important to address for your present and future success.

- **Stopping short of necessary probing.**
  For some reason, people think they've done enough, and can't find anything interesting. Asking and answering the question is getting boring.

  I urge you not stop the process of asking and answering this question too soon. Answer the question at least 10 times, until something juicy and unexpected pops up. One of my students found their nugget of gold at answer 26. Be creative in continuing to ask the question in different ways. For instance, if one of your answers on the first round is "because I don't have time," ask the question differently: "So why am I unwilling to make time for this?" Keep going deeper and deeper. A charge in your body will tell you when you hit pay dirt.

- **Investing too heavily in getting it "right."**
  Pay attention to any sense of desperation to be, do, or have what you

want. In the same way, be patient with your efforts to solve your "problem," or to uncover your unwillingness.

The questions are intentionally repetitive and overlapping. When you are really ready, the answers will appear to you. Be gentle with yourself. As Tara Brach, a Buddhist teacher, reminds us: "Our most direct way of promoting healing and peace is to become mindful of our habits of judging and blaming." Allow yourself to be slow, confused, or even "wrong" along the way.

Summarize your "unwillingness" as best you can

Question Three, our next in this series, will help you resolve your objections. To prepare for this step, it's important to be as clear as you can be about how your current unwillingness blocks you from moving forward. Make a simple, crisp, and succinct summary statement. Be very specific—as embarrassing as it might be. These templates may assist you.

- The reason I'm not doing what I say I want to do more of is my fear that...
- The reason I'm not doing what I say I want to do more of is my belief that...
- The reason I'm not doing what I say I want to do more of is my belief that I am not worthy to....
- The reason I'm not doing what I say I want to do more of is my belief that I don't know how to...
- The reason I'm not doing what I say I want to do more of is my belief that I don't deserve to...

Don't overlook the real possibility that the reason you're not doing what you say you want to do more of....is...actually, deeply, that it is not truly your calling in the world. You may still be working inadvertently with "shoulds" and "oughts" of the past, rather than your true gifts. If that explanation rings true as a reason, rather than as an excuse, sit with it. Be gentle with yourself. Out of that acceptance may spring a new direction for your inquiry.

Having illuminated the misalignments, the blocks, the objections, or the "unwillingnesses," you have made an important step in preparing to let them go. It is important to honor their existence. It is also important to have compassion for yourself for the blocks and barriers you have encountered. After all, you are human. These old beliefs, energetic scripts, or obstacles that you have just named are very powerful. They've had a role in your life, and you can decide to what extent you want them to continue to have such an influential role in the new life you are designing for yourself.

As we come to the end of this chapter, I am aware that a small number of readers may find themselves choosing to back away from doing more of what they love, or from serving in ways that would nourish them. If you are one of those, relax. Allow that the objections you uncovered may be overwhelming and scary. If that is so, at least you can retreat with more awareness of the conflicts you feel, and with the possibility of reevaluating your choice at a later time. Whether you move forward or take another pause with what you have learned in this chapter, please allow your insights to continue to open new doors for your explorations.

In the next chapter, we will look at those objections with new eyes. As Dianne Connolly, co-founder of Tai Sophia, has always said: "Conclusions [read beliefs, objections, or closely held perspectives] are a necessity. They close or open life for ourselves and others. The key is to be awake to them, and to notice that **they are only one way of looking at things.**"

CHAPTER 17

QUESTION THREE:
How Can I Transform My Beliefs?

*"It's not our thoughts, but our attachment to our thoughts,
that causes suffering."*
—*Byron Katie*

BELIEFS ARE POWERFUL. They can sabotage the life you want, and they can energize your possibilities. How do we neutralize the former and promote the latter? As you do the work of Question Three, you have the opportunity to metaphorically chip away and free yourself from the marble that wasn't the David, referenced in the story about Michelangelo. You have the opportunity to free yourself from the erroneous beliefs that are not who you are. You have an opportunity to transform the "unwillingnesses" that may have surprised you into beliefs that will carry you forward. We've entered the arena of potential transformation. Hopefully we can also hold this space as one which accommodates—along with some hard work—some laughter, and some creative play.

It takes courage to admit "unwillingness," and to illuminate your hesitations and objections to moving forward. With Question Three, we will explore ways to let go of, neutralize, and transform those conflicting energies—the ones that typically block forward progress. To get ready for your work, reread the summary of your objections, fears, and beliefs that you developed at the end of Chapter 16. Select one and write it down.

Before we start working with it, however, I want to give an additional personal example to show you where we are going with this process. This story from my youth demonstrates a) a typical source of conflicting energies, b) how beliefs come to be strongly held and not very useful, and c) how they represent, in the simplest sense, old "ideas" and perceived "truths" about ourselves which we can update.

> When I was eight, my mother sent me to a nearby overnight camp. To be perfectly fair, I probably wanted to go. Once there, however, I became ill, and the camp nurse sent me home to recover. Being young and shy and homesick, when I actually recovered, I didn't want to return to camp. I begged and pleaded with my mother to keep me at home. My mother insisted that I return. For other youngsters, the experience of having wishes ignored in that way might not have been traumatic in the scheme of things. For me, it was devastating: a part of me really went into hiding. I concluded at a deep level that my feelings were not important, that no one would listen to me, and that my ideas were not worthy. These beliefs have haunted me and constrained me, lifelong. What I didn't understand for many years, until I recalled this incident in a therapeutic setting, is that **these conclusions were mine alone. While I had adopted them as "true" about me, they were not true—not even in that one moment—nor with that one person.** They were my conclusions, my perceptions of what had happened in that moment and why.

With time and awareness, I have released my grip on those debilitating thoughts, but I notice that they still occasionally waft in my direction. When I get stuck trying to express myself on these pages, I will hear the familiar refrains: "Who are you to think you have something to say?" "Who cares what you think?"

If you are still being hurt by an event that happened to you at twelve, it is the thought that is hurting you now.

— JAMES HILLMAN —

Fortunately, I recognize these thoughts as leftovers from an earlier age. They reflect "truths or conclusions once held." I also recognize they are no longer useful to me, and I choose not to give them power: I reframe them and move on. The "truth," or belief, or conclusion that is more real and more useful to me right now is: "This is an important part of my life's work, and I am privileged to speak it and share it, no matter what anyone else thinks."

We all have beliefs about ourselves and our possibilities. Some of them really support us, like "I'm capable and confident and I can do anything in the world that I choose to do." Some of them—like, "I can't _____ (fill in the blank)"—don't do us any favors.

In my work as a teacher and coach over the years, I have noticed that people who have trouble moving into their ideal work sometimes share the belief that, "Life is hard." Or, "I don't deserve to have my life be so easy and fun (such as it would be if I were doing all that I love.)" Although those may not be the exact beliefs you uncovered in the last chapter, it may be useful to be aware that messages from your past, the ones which serve you and the ones which need to be updated, will likely surface. For now, just pay attention to them and perhaps even write them down for later contemplation.

HOW CAN I TRANSFORM MY BELIEF?

Working with strategies for transforming a belief

Let's get back to the belief or debilitating objection you selected and wrote down earlier. Your job is to apply the following strategies (and there are several with which to experiment), and play with the notion of making the shift for yourself.

1. **Highlight your belief, talk to it, and let it go**, as did Susan, the insurance agent and business owner previously mentioned. She realized that her belief that, "I will dishonor my father's accomplishments by surpassing them" was an unnecessary and self-imposed ceiling to her possibilities. She reevaluated her situation and determined that she could still be loyal and respectful to her father by being as successful as he'd want her to be.

LOOKING AT YOUR OWN EXAMPLE, where do you need to reevaluate and recognize that some conclusion you developed as a child no longer needs to have influence over your behavior?

2. **Craft the more useful truth,** sometimes called an "affirmation," even if you don't believe it at the moment. An affirmation is a positive statement about what you'd like to happen or to be true for you, as if it already were. Susan might say to herself: "I respect and love my father and show it by being as successful as my dreams allow." Or, in the case of my earlier personal example, one of the statements I made to myself, "My feelings matter and I am free to share them with ease—with anyone."

You can repeat the phrase through the discomfort, tears, and the initial embarrassment of feeling like you may be "lying" to yourself. You can state the newly desired version over and over and over until you reach the other side, when it begins to gather its own traction and opens up new and wider possibilities and options. I have used the word "play" intentionally in this process. You can get amazingly creative with affirmations which are designed to derail your mind from its habitual rut. See Appendix B for some more resources and examples on this topic.

LOOKING AT YOUR OWN EXAMPLE, what would be more useful for you to believe about yourself or your situation?

3. **Use several strategies at once.** For instance, you can devise some behaviors to confront your fears or beliefs. Here's an example:

Many people are constrained by a hidden fear of success. Joanna, an owner of a small consulting service, did three things to bring her more comfort with feeling and knowing that it was safe to be successful doing what she loved.

- She recited a new phrase to herself regularly, even though it initially felt very uncomfortable: I am now willing to be successful doing what I love.

- She disciplined herself to name 3 small successes a day (difficult at first) until she got used to the idea, and her sense of herself as being a more successful human being began to flow more easily. (Note: Play is really essential here. When Joanna first started the process, she could only deal with something like, "I didn't spill coffee on my blouse today.")

- She "treated" herself regularly in small ways that she hadn't been accustomed to—a spa visit, a museum visit, a weekend away.

With time, she inexpensively created for herself the habits of "the successful life." As she became comfortable with a more positive view of self, her business began to respond and garnered more clients who wanted to do business with her.

GIVEN YOUR EXAMPLE, what might be some strategies to confront and challenge what you believe about yourself?

Over my lifetime, I have not been exempt from needing to experiment with many new behaviors to confront and neutralize beliefs that did not serve me. Here's another personal example which illustrates the power of challenging experiments.

I grew up in a very thrifty family—New England-born and bred. "We always had enough," a belief which has supported me to this day. But the idea of a luxury purchase usually brought a parental thumbs down.

Later in life, I ran my business on a shoestring. Tired of living on the edge, I chose to confront my belief that I was not deserving of abundance in my business and personal life. I followed my teacher's instruction and gave myself the assignment to take an airline trip—with a first-class reservation. After demonstrating ambivalence about my own deservedness by making, canceling and remaking the reservation about 3 times, I finally surrendered to whatever lesson I was about to learn and confirmed my ticket. A good lesson it was! I learned that I belonged in the first-class cabin as much as anyone else I enjoyed the first-class attention. I realized that while I totally deserved it and could opt for it any time I chose, I concluded that there were many other priorities on which I really preferred to spend my disposable income.

For me, being able to take the first-class experience out of the realm of "I don't deserve" and place it into the realm of "I have the means to make a choice here" constituted an extraordinary release of old emotional baggage. It was worth every penny of that first class ticket.

Dr. Albert Ellis, the renowned founder of Rational Emotive Behavior Therapy (**www.rebt.org**), was a genius at devising new behaviors that would challenge people to release their grip on deeply held, obsessive and immobilizing beliefs. He tells of prescribing a person who suffered by having to be "perfect" to go to work wearing one black shoe and one brown shoe. He once prescribed the person who suffered from fear of being judged as foolish to put a banana on a leash and take it for a walk down a New York City street. Dr. Ellis was known for making up songs which made fun of beliefs that were not useful—like "I have to be perfect," and, "I'm not good enough." You have to laugh, and laughter is a wonderful healing release for fear.

4. **Consider getting professional help if you feel stuck** on certain issues. Confronting the " stuff" you actually believe about yourself is tough, even when it doesn't serve you. And it is probable that the deeper the childhood trauma or wound, the deeper the belief is embedded in your psyche. It is hard to remember it is just "stuff" that can be replaced and updated by new and more useful "stuff." That's why a coach or a therapist can be useful. They can state more useful truths that, in your current state of believing, may not occur to you at all.

Years ago, I received an "out of the blue" call from a local therapist whom I did not know. She asked me me rather abruptly, "What on earth are you doing in those classes you teach?" Her client, and to this day I do not know who she was, was also one of my students. She stated, "Since she has been in your class, she is making progress by leaps and bounds." While I was pleasantly surprised, I didn't know quite what to say.

What I do believe is that when people understand the content and the power of their self-created objections, and understand ways to shift them, they are more able to make good use of professional help.

I believe this was what was happening. My student had sufficient information about her internal process to make her desired change. In this way, she could fully partner with her therapist on her own behalf. We all need support, and I'm glad my student found it in more than one place.

As you work to confront, neutralize, and shift old beliefs, here are some considerations that may help you along the way.

1. **Know that you can update an earlier, less useful belief to one that will be more useful for you as an operating principle.**

Remember that most of our beliefs (useful or less useful) originate in childhood, and describe what we assumed to be true for our lives back then. Without our explicit permission, their influence may still be extending into the present. Do you recognize any of the following beliefs? If so, do you remember when and why you may have decided that one or more of the following was real and true for you?

- Money is hard to come by
- I have to do it all myself
- The world is not safe for me to be who I am
- Life is hard
- I never have enough time

- I'm too young to be credible
- I'm too old to be taken seriously
- My needs are not important enough to take seriously

Or, conversely:

- There's always enough money for my needs
- I always feel supported by others
- My world is safe for me and my ideas
- Life is a wonderful combination of joys and pains
- I have plenty of time for what I want to do
- What I know, I know. I'm eager to share. I'll attract those who are interested in what I know
- My needs are part of my life-giving energy. I honor them

Depression babies of the '20s and '30s who are today's older grandparents provide a wonderful example of some of the beliefs listed in the first grouping. They lived through tough times. Life was really hard. There wasn't enough money. But today, circumstances have changed. Many are still alive, still pinching pennies, avoiding any luxury to the point of obsession, still practicing ingrained habits based on the fears of earlier years.

Although we may deeply believe our constructs and can recite a detailed rationale for our conclusions, that doesn't mean that they are based in today's reality. And most importantly, it doesn't mean they are helpful to us now. They described our conclusions about life back then, but as adults, we do not need to retain those conclusions.

Have some fun reevaluating your early conclusions; have compassion for the difficulties of adults with whom you grew up; shift the beliefs you adopted at an earlier time if they no longer serve you; and begin believing what could be more usefully true about you.

> Feelings that are denied cannot be released; feelings imprison us until they are acknowledged.
>
> — AEESHAH CLOTTEY —

2. **Be gentle on yourself if emotion arises** when you walk the bridge from the older, less useful constructs to the newer, more useful ones. Don't be afraid.

Let me give you another example from my own life of one way this can work. It's a simple one and perhaps a superficial one, but it was profound for me at the time, and it does illustrate the process of walking the bridge to the other side of the belief polarity, accompanied by some intense and very temporary emotional reactions.

One day, many years ago, I received a phone call from someone asking me to write an article for a magazine. I agreed, but with some trepidation. I hadn't a clue about what I might write nor whether I was competent enough to do it. My old reliable nemesis appeared as I listened to myself thinking, "No one wants to know what I have to say. I don't know what to write."

I admit I spent a few moments in fear, totally blocked, until I reminded myself: "You teach this Martha, you ought to use your own technology for this issue. After all, they asked you to do this because they knew you had something to say on the topic. You ought to be able to coax that knowledge out into the open."

Keep in mind that I was feeling unworthy and incompetent, and those judgments about myself FELT ABSOLUTELY TRUE in that moment. I was sure I had nothing to say, and I didn't know what to write. However, there was the MORE USEFUL belief hanging out as another option. I reasoned to myself: "They called me, after all. I do have something to say, and I do know how to say it." Even though I didn't feel this at all at the moment, it was an equally valid construct that would be more useful to have in the driver's seat.

So I put the new, more useful belief in the driver's seat. With great discomfort and many tears, I consciously confronted the existing felt "truth" with the equally valid and, for the moment, newly crafted "truth." I starting saying out loud, "I do know what to write. I'm the only one who knows what to write. It's easy for me to think about what needs to be said." I walked myself over the bridge repeating this phrase through my tears and through the strong feeling that I was in fact "nuts" and just lying to myself, and that this process of mine would never work. I repeated it and repeated it and cried the temporary conflict out of my system. Within 10 minutes, I was on the other side of the dilemma with the more useful truth now operational. I got up to get a pencil and outlined the article then and there, and wrote it the next day with complete ease.

3.   **Understand how insidious and all-pervasive beliefs can be.**

We see the world through our beliefs; we confuse them with the facts of the matter. Consider the oft-told story of the Maine farmer.

> A COUPLE WAS DRIVING THE BACK ROADS looking to buy a home in which to retire. They saw a farmer sitting on the porch and stopped to inquire: "What are the people like in this area?" The old farmer asked: "What are they like where you come from?" The couple replied: "They are cynical and small-minded." The farmer answered, "Well, that's pretty much what they are like here, too."
>
> The next day, another couple came by with the same question. The farmer asked them about the people in their old town. "They're interesting, honest and I'll miss them," was the reply. The farmer replied: "That's what people are like here, too. You'll have great neighbors."

Each couple had formed conclusions about the character of the neighborhoods they were leaving. Neither couple would ever have guessed they were likely to repeat their habitual ways of seeing the world in their new location.

The same is true for you as you look at the "beliefs" you have adopted. It is important to remember that they are your personal constructions and that they will drive all your experiences of life until you change them.

4. **Recognize that your beliefs have been operative throughout this process.**

Some of your beliefs may already have interfered with your process of engagement with the material in this book. If you felt any hesitancy around your answers in the previous explorations, particularly Part Two, see if you can attribute it to something you brought to the table from your past.

5. **Acknowledge that all the "truths" and their "opposite truths" are inside of us.**

We have a choice where to place our focus. There are times we are incompetent and times we are competent, depending on the activity and the hour of the day. We feel smart and we also feel stupid. We are enough and we are also insufficient, depending on the occasion. There are examples of support for us in the world, and there are examples of non-support, depending on where we choose to focus.

In another very common example, we have time (we have all the time there is, 24 hours each day), and we don't have time (those 24 hours may never feel like enough). Both sides of the statements can qualify, in any given moment, as "our perceived truth" about the situation in which we find ourselves. I would not hesitate to claim that focusing on and operating with the notion that "I have time" will typically result in more calmness and less stress.

The challenge is always to choose the most useful position on which to stand, and to operate "as if," despite the fact that we might temporarily be concerned that we are "lying" to ourselves.

Common pitfalls—in no particular order

The Primary Pitfall: Giving up on the process.

Many people conclude that repeating newly minted positive statements, sometimes called affirmations, don't work.

When someone tells me this, I tend to agree. It usually means that the statement they happen to be using will not necessarily work for the issue they are trying to shift. In many of the popular books on affirmations, you can find an abundance of generic statements that will work for some people sometimes, and not for others. See Appendix B for more resources on affirmations.

Expecting too much too soon.

Yes, when we are diligent about our analysis and craft new practices, we do so with high hopes and deep wishes for fast results.

I don't believe that shifting deeply held beliefs about who you are, and the possibilities you have, is an easy task. Discovering, refining and reversing one's internal infrastructure takes time. This pitfall is thinking that a moment of making a positive statement will resolve things immediately. Be patient and keep holding to your new and more useful ideas and practices.

Taking it all too seriously.

It does seem very serious. You are looking at your life deeply. You are facing the need to reevaluate core operating principles of your life. For instance, if your life has been based on "I am not good enough," it is hard to make the shift to a more self-affirming position and hard to take it lightly.

On the other hand, you are not alone. Might you dare laugh about the foibles of being human that so many of us share? Might you make a game of beginning to treat yourself well in small ways? A la Albert Ellis, might you make fun of your particularly onerous belief in song? Laughter works.

Not asking for help when you need reassurance.

Making significant change is never really easy. Something ends and needs to be grieved. Something new is emerging and needs to be accommodated.

It is not unusual for people going through this process to enter a period of feeling down and confused. While this is certainly no fun, the good news is that it means the process is working. Just keep going. The old and the new parts of you are fighting it out—and you are in charge of who gets the upper hand.

This kind of reassurance is often all one needs. You can expect some emotional bumps when you move from thinking in an old way to thinking in a new way. The normal phenomenon you will experience of temporary loss, sadness and confusion does not need to be held as serious clinical depression.

If you find you would like the reassurance and guidance of a trained person to help you get through this stage, by all means, seek it. The right helper will understand and honor the natural, albeit emotionally confusing, process that occurs when one is taking significant growth steps and leaving a part of her- or himself behind.

Not remembering that emotional reactions are both likely and temporary.

Dark nights often precede the breakthrough into a new day. It is the nature of the hero's and heroine's journey, captured in many of our Greek myths. Our heroes/heroines must go to the depths and ask for help before they receive the reward they seek.

Getting lost in your "stuff."

In the midst of change, sometimes it feel like the anchor is not holding and you have lost your compass. But life goes on.

You can do this journey, and you can still live your life. Be sure to take time out to smell the roses, nurture yourself, play with your children, and kiss your spouse. Stay in charge; you are bigger than your temporary emotional turmoil. Be the witness on your own shoulder: you can watch the journey unfold and stay present in the rest of your life, too.

One more thing about the "Big Nudge..."

Some people reaching this point may feel overwhelmed by the idea that they might have to spend years in therapy to exorcize the myriad of beliefs that are not aligned with their moving forward in life. The "years" part is less true than it was once believed to be.

Here's the bottom line:

- Negativity and stress of any kind, at the conscious level or the unconscious level, block creativity. They also block liveliness, health and wellness, relationships, and our ability to access the many good ideas and energetic vibrations that are out there for our benefit.

- For ease of entry into the life and work one loves, negativity about new possibilities does need to be addressed, overridden, neutralized, and shifted. A new script needs to be written.

- There are many new therapeutic modalities emerging in the world of energy medicine. They can help you do this work more easily and more quickly than you might imagine. Look in Appendix C for a sampling of approaches. All have websites offering information through books, tapes, DVDs, and workshops. Many offer free newsletters and free basic instructions.

- Once you have "named" the blocks and barriers within you and identified some of their sources, I believe these emerging therapies offer a good and efficient path for working through personal changes and supporting the life you are wanting to create.

You have now engaged with the Three Questions. Through them, you have discovered what may—or may not—be required of you as you follow your desires, take action, and do more of what you love—in your life and in your community.

Anticipating change and beginning to practice new behaviors almost always bring up fear. You can either succumb to fear or you can befriend it. You can unearth the beliefs that source the fear, have fun with them, and have a different kind of conversation with yourself. It is your choice.

When you are ready to move on, Part Five offers inspiration from others who have taken action and found their new work or their next work. Their lives may offer suggestions for your own next steps.

In the meantime, it's time for another pause!

Reflection

You have goals, desires, and gifts—and you want to exercise them. You also know now that you may be standing, or sitting, in your own way. This recognition can set you free and propel you to make some changes in the way you think about your situation. Welcome to the human race. You have many aspects to your personality, some of which may distress you and others of which may delight you.

How are you feeling?

— Get a cup or tea or coffee, find a quiet spot, sit down.

— Appreciate that there is nothing to do right now.

— Take a long slow deep breath.

We're taking a little break for some reflection.

• What surprised you about your discoveries?

• What are you learning that is going to require either patience or curiosity on your part?

And most important...

What's becoming clear to you?

PART FIVE

It's Time to Act

IT'S TIME TO ACT

YES, IT'S TIME TO GET INTO ACTION! Because some sort of action will be required to express yourself in the world. Or, at least some sort of different actions than you have been doing.

I have spent my days stringing and unstringing my instrument, while the song I came to sing remains unsung.

— RABINDRANATH TAGORE —

When it came to writing this part, I confess I encountered a new ambivalence in myself. All my life, I have been a planner, a doer, a problem-solver, an activator, a Queen of the To-Do List. That said, I'm now noticing that as I've gotten older, I've found myself questioning my form of "doing." The "forced marches" on which I used to send myself no longer seem to resonate with the joy, ease and flow that I associate with "calling."

As I look back, writing this book had a flow of its own. One day I simply started writing. The purpose and the title evolved and changed several times. Many ideas appeared in serendipitous conversations, in unexpected emails, in the text of a song at a concert, in a magazine at my doctor's office. Others simply popped into my head, or landed on my radar screen, when the time to write about them arrived.

While this is not the book I started out to write, I have been surprised and pleased at the ease of the process, and at my growing willingness to follow the path as it emerged. Apparently, holding my focus on expressing what matters to me and letting go of trying to force the direction of this book is what has brought it to life.

For the last 18 months, I have noticed that I no longer carry my once-trusty "to do" list. While I am not sure what that is about, I notice that I have also developed an aversion to my lifelong habit of creating checklists to map out each activity of the day. As a result, Part Five, the part of the book that might be expected to contain the checklists for action, has very few of them.

What it does have is twelve short chapters, each an observation of how someone entered or refined their calling journey. That's as close to an action guide as I will offer you. Maybe they will serve as twelve suggestions, or twelve models, or twelve ideas in no particular order. In any case, the time has come to think about getting into your own act!

How *will* you start to do more of what you love? What will you do next to deepen the path you are on?

If you have really done the work of discovering what you want your life to be about...

If you have unearthed your own beliefs about the possibility or impossibility of making that happen...

If you have reevaluated and refined your inner alignment with your intentions...

...then you are ready to get into action. When you clarify your intent, and surrender to what may be possible, the next steps have a tendency to appear on their own.

> A year from now you may have wished you started today.
>
> — SAMUEL JOHNSON

Thus, in Part Five, I primarily show real people moving forward and finding ways to do more of what they love. A thirteenth chapter encourages you to find your own way. That's because, while the twelve ideas presented may be useful, they certainly do not exhaust the world of possibilities for actually making something happen. I'm trusting that you, too, will find your own unique way to get started expressing in the world the calling that lives within you.

This means going with the flow—and listening to your own best wisdom and expertise. There are many ways to follow up and follow through. Providing you have done your personal work along the lines suggested in this book, or with other guides of your choice, I can guarantee that, without much effort on your part, some of what you want and need will one day land on your doorstep, ring your doorbell, and say, "Here I am." It may not land with trumpets blaring, but one day you'll wake up and notice, "Hey, look at my life. This is just what I was meant to be doing."

So here we are. We live in a world where we have the leverage to make things happen, the desire to do work we believe in, and a marketplace that is begging us to be remarkable.

— SETH GODIN —

CHAPTER 18

❧

Stop Doing What You Don't Want to Do!

"I merely took the energy it takes to pout and wrote the blues."
—*Duke Ellington*

EACH TIME I MENTION THE TITLE for this book, acquaintances and strangers alike give me heartfelt responses. One woman sadly recounted the story of her husband who, for a large part of his life, felt trapped in a job he didn't love. He felt overwhelmed with the "duty" to provide an education for his children. This was despite his wife's assurances that she would be happy to make changes in their lifestyle so that he could do something more professionally satisfying. Now a widow, she still carries regrets about that aspect of their life together.

If you happen to be one of those people who feel trapped, here's an idea you may want to consider before going further. One of my serendipitous encounters was with Tim Frangioso, 35, who had been miserable in a corporate job. He agonized about his options before he finally made a change.

Although Tim's friends thought he had really "made it" in his well-paying, high-tech job, he was actually "dying." For several years, he was so fearful of giving up the cushy paycheck, the lifestyle, and the benefits that he, too, tried to persuade himself that he had "made it." It was his wife who, tired, frustrated, and unhappy after six years of living with the shadow of the man she loved, finally, in his own words, "pushed me off the cliff."

Tim quit. He started fresh. He began to figure out what he wanted. He became a realtor, and his wife followed suit. Finally, after years of a heavy international travel schedule, Tim and his wife could enjoy being home together, working and making a living in their community.

That's not the end of the story, however. Selling houses was Tim's finely honed skill, but not his calling. Selling houses happened to be the vehicle by which he exercised his calling to teach, motivate, serve others, and build community. He taught new realtor certification programs. He set up an informal weekly teaching/learning forum for solo professionals like himself who tend to feel lonely and isolated.

The goals of these meetings were for members to learn from Tim, and to support and learn from each other. A direct byproduct was also the personal nourishment that comes from being with other like-minded small business people. One attendee, Paul Stallman from Alias Solutions, found the meetings so valuable that he crafted a subscription website for Tim at **www.tuesdaymorningswithtim.com**. On that site, out-of-towners can access the information, videos, PowerPoint presentations, and discussions.

Obviously, Tim's relationships, formed in that breakfast nook, also generate leads for his real estate business. This is an effortless byproduct of his being out in the world as a person who gives value and service. But as Tim summarizes, "What's most important is that there is not one day in the last six years that I haven't enjoyed getting out of bed in the morning. I'm doing what I love. I know my business will not thrive unless I continue to learn from others, and help them to thrive, as well. It's that second role where I am most happy and creative!"

Tim's very simple guidance to anyone who asks how he did it: "If you don't like what you are doing—Stop! If you want to do something else—Start!"

ADDITIONAL RESOURCES YOU MAY ENJOY

Tribes: We Need YOU to Lead Us by Seth Godin, 2008. You can also subscribe to the inspirational daily blog about being effective in the world. **Visit www.SethGodin.com.**

CHAPTER 19

Lean into the 'Yes'

"The best time to plant a tree was always 20 years ago.
The second best time is always today."
—*Chinese Proverb*

MY FRIEND CHRISTINE, in her 50s, her children off to college, was thinking about what she wanted to do next with her life. A dedicated musician, she held the volunteer post of music minister at our small interfaith community church, thoughtfully selecting the hymns and chants and preludes to enrich our services. She also held paid chorus assignments in other locations. Like many curious and active people with a passion for life, she had explored many fields, among them becoming trained as an Alexander Technique (bodywork) practitioner.

I found her recent announcement at church quite intriguing. She said, "I want you all to know that I am finally accepting my 'calling' as a piano teacher."

In our conversation after the service, she added: "As soon as I made this commitment to follow my heart, my supply of Alexander students abruptly dried up, and my piano student population continues to grow, easily and effortlessly. I've even had to turn down requests for lessons and set up a waiting list."

In another conversation six months later, Christine said her piano practice was still going strong. She told me more about just feeling the "call" and being willing to say "yes" to it, without knowing exactly how it was going to work out. Judging from Christine's experience, I think it fair to conclude that when you are exercising your true gifts, what you give is returned to you multiplied. When you are aligned with your work, in body, mind and spirit, the forces of the universe conspire to applaud you and support you. That's just the way it works.

Saying "yes" to that which is alive within you is a power move of the best kind.

ADDITIONAL RESOURCES YOU MAY ENJOY

The Answer to How is Yes: Acting on What Matters
by Peter Block, 2002

CHAPTER 20

Start Somewhere

"Don't let life discourage you; everyone who got where he is had
to start where he was."
—*Lao-Tzu*

SOMETIMES, YOU JUST HAVE TO START WHEREVER YOU ARE,
and share your passion.

As my radar became set to calling and contribution, wonderful examples
came to my attention. One day in March 2009, National Public Radio broad-
cast an interview with Eric Schwartz, the co-founder of Citizen Schools.
Eric's simple idea provided ways for people to share their passions, find more
meaning in their own lives, and make a real and necessary contribution to
children. Here's their story in brief, liberally quoted from their website and
links. **Visit www.citizenschools.org.**

In Boston in 1994, the downward spiral of crumbling neighborhoods,
youth crime, and struggling public schools presented opportunities awaiting
discovery. That summer, social entrepreneurs Eric Schwartz and Ned Rimer
understood three important factors:

- Children faced long, empty hours outside of school
- Middle school can be a crucial transition in a child's education
- Real-world professionals can have a powerful impact on students by
  sharing their knowledge in a hands-on format

They began an experiment.

Both men volunteered to teach twenty 5th grade students for the summer at Dorchester's Paul A. Dever School. Eric, a former reporter, with a
Masters degree in Education from Harvard, taught journalism. Ned, a former

Emergency Medical Technician squad chief, taught first aid. They called themselves Citizen Teachers. Neither could have predicted the response of the children, how much they would learn, or how much they themselves would love the project.

This was a simple idea, born of the gifts of Schwartz and Rimer, exercised in the right time and the right place. Among their gifts were a pioneering passion and a deep appreciation of a teacher's capacity for changing the lives of children. To this, they added their love of relating to middle school children and the desire to make a difference. Add, too, their business and entrepreneurial abilities to craft a simple model with political appeal.

Today Citizen Schools, with Schwartz as CEO, operates in 37 middle schools in seven states, serving 4,000 kids in afterschool programs, and engaging 4,000 volunteers in the service of educating youth and strengthening communities. What attracts the volunteers?

"I wanted to give something back!"

"I love to teach what I love!"

"It makes me feel good about myself to know I've had a role in making a child feel better about him or herself!"

It's important not to make this all seem too simple. However, it is good to remember that it started with two people who had an idea and wanted to make a difference in children's education. They decided to conduct an experiment in educational reform.

It began with the two of them selling the idea of volunteering to teach something they loved and were good at. Their continued success depended not only on the enthusiastic results they got from children and families, but also upon other citizen experts who volunteered to not only teach what they loved, but to serve as caring adults in the lives of middle school children for one day a week. What a win-win-win: for the schools, the children, and the volunteers.

Above all, they tapped this array of talent and expertise with a very simple challenge: two tutors, one summer. They started somewhere!

ADDITIONAL RESOURCES YOU MAY ENJOY

Letters To A Young Teacher by Jonathon Kozol, 2008
And any other book by Jonathon Kozol, activist and educator

CHAPTER 21

❧

Reinforce Your Own Clarity

"Vision is the art of seeing the invisible."
—*Jonathan Swift*

REINFORCE YOUR OWN CLARITY! For what you are wanting, of course. On a daily basis! This is an affirmative technique for staying focused. I have helped people adopt this across 30 years, and most continue to find it helpful. Reinforcing clarity for the positive on a daily basis is a way to strengthen your intentions and magnetize energy on your own behalf.

For instance, craft a statement, sometimes called an affirmation, which states very simply what you are wanting as if you already have it. For instance, "The right helper comes into my life easily." Or, "I find it easy to prepare nutritious meals for myself and my family."

I underscore focusing on the positive, as it is amazing how quickly we can slip into a negative frame. For instance, "What I want is not to have trouble finding good employees." Or, "I wish I liked to cook good food."

One summer, I had a life-changing experience with the power of establishing and reinforcing the kind of positive, no-nonsense clarity I'm talking about. While Lynn Graborn's book listed below will give you more in-depth information and examples, let me first share a personal experience about coming to clarity.

It was the month of June. Being in business for myself had been stressful. I was in conflict: I longed for a summer off and I also wanted a big contract that would help me feel comfortable about taking time off. Turning to my familiar practice of affirmative intention, I alternated between two: "I now have time to rest and relax," and, "I easily receive a large work contract."

This didn't go well. When I gave attention to the affirmative intention for a summer off, I'd hear the "but, but, but" in my mind arguing that I didn't have the money to allow that. When I gave attention to my desire for a big contract, I'd hear the "but, but, but" argument that I was tired and needed time off. The conflict wore me down.

One day I realized that what I *really* wanted was both. **I wanted to feel totally and abundantly supported in taking time off.** Finally at peace, I set my intentions to the certainty of that possibility: *"I am now abundantly supported in taking the time I need for me."* I put out an emotional welcome mat for the realization of financial support for time off. I affirmed for all things good in my life.

Within two weeks, a response arrived. I received a request in the mail for contract work from a client to **begin in September**. This was work that had neither been proposed by me nor previously requested by the client. When I called my client to inquire, she said: "I was just doing my planning for next fiscal year, and making some year-end commitment of funds. I hope you can do the work."

Since I have no other explanation for these events, I give credit to my having created personal clarity and an energy of welcome. In any case, I just said: "Thank you."

The lesson? Do what you need to do to become clear and unconflicted about what you want—so that your affirmation of your committed intention can magnetize the possibilities you hope to bring into reality.

ADDITIONAL RESOURCES YOU MAY ENJOY

Excuse Me, Your Life is Waiting: The Astonishing Power of Feelings by Lynn Grabhorn, 2003. In this book, the author describes in great detail how to use the technique of "buzzing" affirmatively for what you want.

CHAPTER 22

❧

Follow Your Heart

*"I'd rather be a failure at something I enjoy than a success
at something I hate."*
— George Burns

FOR THOSE OF US WHO MAY BE INTIMIDATED by the thought of
playing in the big leagues, my observation is that everything starts small.
With one choice. A heartfelt choice.

I have set my radar to notice people who live their calling, and whose
contributions ripple out around them. Many have appeared on my screen.
One reliable source of people who are doing what they love has been the
weekly magazine of our regional newspaper. Each week, the magazine profiles
a member of the local community. I began to see, over and over again,
quotes like: "This where I am meant to be." " I love what I am doing and
can't imagine doing anything else." Hmmmm. I decided to pay closer attention to the profiles.

Betty Thayer had a work history that ultimately led her to a place where
she could say: "I love every minute of it. I'm doing what I was meant to do
and making a difference in my client's lives." Her early choices to be a caretaker were replicated by similar choices as her life progressed. As a young
mother, she and her husband and their three children shared their home with
a dozen foster children. When the children were in school, she chose to fulfill
a lifelong dream of becoming a nurse. After stints in hospice, in a nursing
home, and as a daycare director for another company, Betty decided to start
her own adult day-care business, **Thayercare, Inc.** The business serves 40–50
adult clients a day. Betty's services allow her clients to continue living at
home, either independently or with family, while relieving family members of
the responsibilities of full-time caretaking.

Betty Thayer's consistent choices over a lifetime, reflected in many forms of caretaking and administrative callings, all coalesced into her current vision of right livelihood. This particular livelihood also happens to contribute abundantly to her community. (Daily Hampshire Gazette, Hampshire Life, April 3, 2009)

Jason Greene started helping his father paint interior and exterior residences in his teen years, and he later painted his way through college. He tried many jobs in his early working career, one of which was with a physical therapy company, which had him living and working in several states. Later, back in Massachusetts, he worked in the rehabilitation department of a local hospital, and also as a salesman for a prosthetic and orthotic company.

He then returned to the career he knew he loved—painting homes—and to a lifestyle that allows him to include other things he loves, like coaching youth sports and spending time with his family. About painting, he says:

"J. Greene Painting is not work to me. It's peaceful, and a passion of mine. I enjoy seeing the transformation of a home, and my reward is a satisfied customer." (Daily Hampshire Gazette, Hampshire Life, March 13, 2009)

While Jason Greene took a more circuitous route in his career than did Betty Thayer, it seems that both listened to their hearts and kept choosing the next right step. Both have ended up in situations where they are able to fully and happily acknowledge a life of calling and contribution.

Two more heart-centered individuals captured my attention.

One, **Andrew DeVries**, dropped out of school at 15 already knowing that he loved to sketch and draw more than anything else. Inspired early in his life by dance and movement, his career path included apprenticeship with a sculptor and study in Paris. His works now grace public institutions across New England and private collections worldwide. His advice to readers: "Know what is in your heart." (Daily Hampshire Gazette, Hampshire Life, May, 2009), **Visit www.andrewdevries.com.**

Another was lifelong railroad buff **Craig Della Penna**. When, in the mid 1990s, he was asked to write a guidebook for rail trails in the Northeastern states, Craig became an advocate for the rebirth of abandoned rail corridors. He saw them carrying cyclists and pedestrians—and connecting communities in the process. An activist with his small consultancy, Northeast Greenway Solutions, and a realtor specializing in antique homes and properties close to trails and greenways, Craig has also created, along with his wife, a bed-and-breakfast inn along the Northampton Bike Path. He closed his interview with the sentiments which basically inspired this book: "I'm just having too much fun and I just might be living your dream life." Gazette Hampshire Life, May 29, 2009. **Visit www.sugar-maple-inn.com.**

Though some of the life choices mentioned above get traction or a business plan and into larger endeavors, all of those individuals mentioned clearly perform deeply satisfying services which ripple out to others in some nourishing way. I thank Steve Pfarrer, whose weekly newspaper column reminds me that contribution and calling are alive and well everywhere you look! I also thank the four individuals for allowing me to share their stories. Hopefully, each story will encourage you, the reader, to keep listening to your heart and following wherever it invites you.

ADDITIONAL RESOURCES YOU MAY ENJOY

A Life at Work: The Joy of Discovering What You Were Born to Do by Thomas Moore. 2008.

This Time I Dance! Creating the Work You Love by Tama J. Kieves, 2007. A career coach tells her story about making the shift from corporate law to something she liked much better, with steps you can follow.

CHAPTER 23

❦

Make Time for Fun

"When people are laughing, they're generally not killing each other."
—*Alan Alda*

MEET THE FLY LADY. Her passion is fishing, hence her nickname. But at one time, her life was messy and chaotic, leaving little time for relaxing with her passion. So she figured out a system to make it better for herself which seemed to work. Then she created a small business which allowed her to share her system with others. And throughout it all, she allowed her quirky, funny personality to predominate. She just had fun.

The core principle of her system is easy. It starts with cleaning the kitchen sink and keeping it spotless. It continues with timed 15-minute, start-any-where, clean-up commitments. When the buzzer goes off, you stop—unless, of course, you are having fun. You can do anything for 15 minutes.

This is her "start somewhere" act. The sink is what is sacred. It's the central promise that seems to ripple out to the rest of the house with ease, assisted by her other useful and easy tips. Just start by cleaning the sink and keeping it spotless! Every single day.

Then came an interesting, quirky, and lively website. She added to this a book and speeches, all of which spread her message. For women (and men) who live in CHAOS (Can't Have Anyone Over Syndrome), her advice is refreshing, funny, and practical, too.

Testimonials for the Fly Lady's approach abound, from reformed packrats to those who formerly spent their mornings in pajamas in front of the TV. Thousands of women report that their home environments now support their goals for health, happiness, family harmony and order. These newly empowered fans inspire each other with their posted letters.

The Fly Lady shares with others her common sense joyfulness, and quirk-iness, and bravely tells the truth about life. She offers funny products, and shares a positive, irrepressible attitude. Above all, she has created something out of her own tough times, discouragement, and broken marriage—and has turned it into a gift for herself and for many others.

The Fly Lady makes money and has fun, all the while helping people deal with real-time issues. She then nudges her flock into their own callings and contributions, as they become freed from disorder and begin to feel better about themselves and their chaos-free homes.

She herself now has a harmonious home, a happy new husband, and reason to be proud of her healthy number of good deeds for humanity.

And, most importantly, she has plenty of time to go fishing.

Although I tend to think that anyone doing what they love is already having fun, there is an extra dimension to the irrepressibility of self that the Fly Lady exhibits. Maybe checking out her business site will encourage you to let loose and have even more fun in your life and work. **Visit www.flylady.net.**

ADDITIONAL RESOURCES YOU MAY ENJOY

"Seven days without laughter makes one weak," says Dr. Joel Goodman, founder and director of The HUMOR Project, in his book, *Laffirmations*. For 40 years, Dr. Goodman has been exercis-ing his own calling by helping people to get more smileage out of their lives and jobs. **Visit www.humorproject.com.** Attend his annual humor conference in Sarasota Springs, New York. It's a real blast!

CHAPTER 24

Bend Those Rules

"To be truly radical is to make hope possible
rather than despair convincing."
—*Raymond Williams*

THERE ARE MANY RULES IN OUR SOCIETY that were created for legitimate purposes. Yet, in certain situations, they simply don't serve the larger objective. When the greater good is at stake, it is important to assume that these "rules" can be adjusted, flexed or bypassed by those who are able to make a difference and who are willing to take the consequences.

Take, for example, a man who was able to use his extraordinary gifts in part because he didn't assume that the rules in the system would be a deterrent. Fortunately, neither did the bureaucrats who created and typically enforced the rules. I am speaking about an educator named Mr. Gunn.*

Mr. Gunn was a security guard at a Midwestern high school. In the 1990s, he volunteered as assistant football coach. Later, when the head coach job came open, he applied and was accepted—despite his lack of teacher certifications. In the capacity of head coach, he used his extraordinary charisma and natural talent to inspire young men, who set winning records both on the team and in the classroom, for a number of years.

Mr. Gunn thought he could do even more. With clarity and enthusiasm, he proposed to set up a charter school for young men who were at risk of failing in school and life. Again, he was seeking this position without the requisite teaching credentials.

Far-sighted administrators saw his talent, his character, and his results. They bent their rules, or made new ones. At the time of the interview, Mr. Gunn headed up an academy for young men at risk without appropriate support and guidance in their lives. His students are already exceeding the average test scores of the public high schools in the urban area in which it is based.

As part of the contract for attending this school, all the students are required to wear bright red jackets daily. Gunn's theory: "Young men at Gunn will stand out. They will be picked on for standing out in this way. And if they are going to be successful in society, they need to learn to stand for something, and to handle what comes."

Kudos to the school administration who recognized that the lack of credentials in Mr. Gunn's resume should not be an impediment to his obvious and unique ability to promote educational excellence among hard-to-reach young men—and getting them off to college.

ADDITIONAL RESOURCES YOU MAY ENJOY

An Unreasonable Woman: A True Story of Shrimpers, Politicos, Polluters, and the Fight for Seadrift, Texas by Diane Wilson, 2005. An amazing and true story of a very smart woman, who, with no formal education, knew right from wrong, and broke all the rules to prevail.

First, Break All the Rules: What the World's Greatest Managers Do Differently by Marcus Buckingham and Curt Coffman, 1999.

---

* Mr. Gunn was featured in a television interview sometime in 2008 and fascinated me. I have been unable to verify the source of this story. I hope that Mr. Gunn will ultimately surface and address any inaccuracies that may exist in this text.

CHAPTER 25

Share With Significants

"People change and forget to tell each other."
—*Lillian Hellman*

WHEN ONE PERSON GROWS AND CHANGES, it impacts relationships with the people who mean the most to them. Keeping significant others informed regarding what is going on with you is often overlooked, partly because sharing your journey, your insights, your fears and your conclusions with important people in your life can be intimidating. On the other hand, the willingness to be vulnerable, to risk being seen for who you really are, can also elicit new perspectives, deeper understanding, and tremendous support. It goes two ways: listening to others' fears and concerns about the changes you are contemplating is an act of respect for any significant people in your life.

Your insistence on stepping out of old habits and moving along the path to doing more of what you love can coexist with the needs and feelings of those around you. As you either inaugurate or continue the conversation you may be having with yourself about your individual need to grow and change, how will you balance your parallel need to stay connected with those you love?

This particular reminder to share with the significants in your life is clearly worth a book of its own. People like Dr. Marshall Rosenberg and his colleagues, referenced below as a resource, have already been "called" to develop and teach heartfelt communication as their lifework. They have already written those books. I mention the point here briefly because it is an important consideration for any action strategy. Changes of any import in your life and work increase the urgency for communication with those around you.

The following quotations invite you to simply remind yourself of the necessity of keeping others up to date with what's going on with you, and to find the courage and skill you may require to reveal your needs and feelings and to listen to those of others.

In the progress of personality,
first comes a declaration of independence,
then a recognition of interdependence.
—*Henry Van Dyke*

We are not the same persons this year as last;
nor are those we love.
It is a happy chance if we, changing,
continue to love a changed person.
—*William Somerset Maugham*

Avoiding danger is no safer in the long run
than outright exposure.
—*Helen Keller*

It's one thing to feel that you are on the right path,
but it's another to think that yours is the only path.
—*Paulo Coelho*

ADDITIONAL RESOURCES YOU MAY ENJOY

Dr. Marshall Rosenberg's Center for Non-Violent Communication offers books, tapes and workshops to enable people to express their own needs and feelings, and to listen to those of others. I highly recommend this resource, the classes and the trained practitioners, for practically every important interaction, including the most contentious. **Visit www.cnvc.org.**

CHAPTER 26

❦

Address Your Own Needs

"If each of us did nothing more than to take responsibility for ourselves, none of us would have to wish that we could change the world."
—*Shad Helmstetter*

SHARON, THE NURSE AT THE SENIOR CENTER who tends my toes, has a full and unheralded life doing what she loves, on a schedule that meets her needs to be the mother and wife she wants to be. I consider her one of my heroines, unknown and unpublished, who has followed her nose to create a life that works for her, her family and her clients. She joins the many other unsung heroes and heroines who dare to choose to make their lives work happily.

It's critical to address your own needs, and to be open to wherever they may take you. Here are four others who, like Sharon, addressed their own needs and made a fulfilling life for themselves and others.

Greg Mortensen, world-class mountaineer, made a simple promise to build a school for members of the Afghan community who had literally saved his life after a climbing injury. But one wasn't enough: having built the one, he was hooked! He ended up being a one-man version of the Peace Corps in Pakistan and Afghanistan. Fifteen years later, he had helped other rural communities build 131 schools. His book, *Three Cups of Tea*, landed on the best-seller lists and helped attract the funds to keep doing what he found he so wanted to keep doing. His book is sitting-on-the-edge-of-one's-chair-fascinating for many reasons—not the least of which is the way he describes making his promise and then figuring out how to keep it, all the while being clueless about how to go about it. His story is yet one more testimony to the power of intention, commitment, and persistence. **Visit www.threecupsoftea.com.**

Colin Beaven, a writer, was getting tired of writing about history, and became much more interested in the issue of global warming. He had a personal and nagging concern that he was part of the problem. So he started making some changes in the way he lived his life. With his wife as partner and ally, they reduced their buying to primarily local food, and used no TV, air conditioners, elevators or subways. In other words, he became an "eco-extremist." He wrote a regular blog about "what each of us can do to end our environmental crisis, make a better place to live for ourselves and everyone else, and hopefully come up with a happier way of life along the way." Throughout the year, in his blog (noimpactman.com), he publicly tracked the living out of his commitment. Subscribers could accompany him on the experiment, learn about his strategies, and share his dilemmas.

At this writing, Colin Beaven, his wife and young daughter have completed their year off the grid. A book and a documentary telling the family's story—what they did and what they learned—both eco-sensitively produced, was released in September 2009. Learn the next iteration of this fascinating experiment addressing one man's burning need to be part of the solution and to understand how more of us could join in the effort. **Visit www.noImpactProject.org.**

Mary Cowhey is a teacher who followed her own inspired common sense about how early childhood education could be at its best—how it could prepare children for the issues and dilemmas of the real world. An educational activist, her mission evolved as she learned how to build social consciousness in her second graders, and then wrote about it. Her experiments and experiences are published in a delightful memoir *Black Ants and Buddhists: Thinking Critically and Teaching Differently in the Primary Grades.* Mary is still teaching in Northampton, Massachusetts, and her book has been added to the reading lists in schools of education. Her experiences provide models to be emulated by all who dare to change the world by building the practical habits of social consciousness in the very young.

Lisa Lillien had a different set of nagging concerns. A successful young career woman, she was plagued by **20** extra pounds that came on, came off, and came on again. Her food and weight life was a struggle. One day in 2002, she said, "Enough!" She turned her food obsession into nutritional research and observation of the foods that triggered her binges. She started preparing snacks and low-calorie recipes for herself. Her family and friends loved it when she shared the results of her investigations and the new recipes she was creating. Ultimately, she quit her job and devoted all her time to her hobby, to see if she could make a go of it. She created a daily email service called HUNGRY GIRL, providing nutritional information, low-calorie snack recipes, and encouragements. By the end of 2009, she expects to have 1,000,000 subscribers.

By her own admission, Lisa is neither a nutritionist nor a health food advocate. She's a formerly pudgy "foodie" who is still continually hungry. Two books later, with Fortune 500 advertisers and the possibility of a TV show, she owns a $2,000,000 business. Having started by meeting her own needs, Lisa is now positioned to have a significant influence on at least some of those struggling with the epidemic of obesity in our country. As of this writing, Lisa is still offering a free subscription to her daily tips for controlling calories.* **Visit www.hungrygirl.com.**

Inspiring people are everywhere, some are very public, others are less known. It's important to understand that the value of a person's calling is not measured by their notoriety. Like Sharon, the Senior Center nurse, these four individuals paid attention to their own needs, desires and interests, and kept following their noses with courage and curiosity and a good dose of commitment. Unlike Sharon, they also wrote about it, or entered the public marketplace. Their stories allow the rest of us to see what's possible.

When we hear stories of people doing good work in the world, seemingly spending all their energy "serving" others, it is easy to miss—and important to remember—that they are also basically meeting their own needs.

It's important to ask: Am I, by any chance, suppressing any of my own un-kept promises? Am I, by any chance, denying any of my own compelling personal interests and needs? Am I, by any chance, ignoring any of my own inspired common sense about what this world needs—and avoiding doing something about it?

Take a moment to think about these questions. Try to uncover and honor your own personal urgings and needs, and lean into them. You have but one life to live. Who knows what you can make happen when you start doing what you need to do for yourself?

ADDITIONAL RESOURCES YOU MAY ENJOY

No Impact Man: The Adventures of a Guilty Liberal Who Attempts to Save the Planet, and the Discoveries He Makes About Himself and Our Way of Life in the Process by Colin Beaven, 2009

Black Ants and Buddhists: Thinking Critically and Teaching Differently in the Primary Grades by Mary Cowhey, 2006. Cowhey's students learn to make connections between their lives, the books they read, the community leaders they meet, and the larger world.

Stones into Schools: Promoting Peace with Books not Bombs, in Afghanistan and Pakistan by Greg Mortenson, 2009 Visit www.penniesforpeace.org.

Start Where You Are: A Guide to Compassionate Living by Pema Chodrun. 1994. One of the popular authors and spokespersons for the Buddhist philosophy of being where you are and doing what's next.

From an article by Rene Lynch for the Los Angeles Times, reprinted in the Daily Hampshire Gazette, Weekend Living, August 1, 2009

CHAPTER 27

❧

Form Alliances

"The power of this new era is simple: If you want to (need to, must!) lead then you can. But if this isn't the right moment, if this isn't the right cause, then hold off. Generous and authentic leadership will always defeat the selfish efforts of someone doing it just because she can."
—*Seth Godin*

WILL YOU BE THE INITIATOR? Or the follower? What's your best role in a team? Leader or team member? Strategist or implementer? Philosopher or problem solver? Each needs the other.

Some people have big ideas—bigger than their natural strengths can accommodate. They need allies, partners, investors, CEOs, CFOs, technicians, helpers, team members, employees, to achieve their goals and make the contribution to which they aspire and of which they are capable. Although big thinkers can often attract allies by the imperatives of their vision, they also need to specify the kinds of help they need, put out the word, welcome it when it shows up, and allow others to actually help.

Joe Edelman of Northampton, MA is one of those visionaries. He remembers writing down a list, at age 16, of all the world's problems that needed solving. As a young adult, Joe went to college and spent time mastering high-tech systems at MIT and in several research laboratories. Now 33, this activist's dream is to recast our social contract with each other. He wants to make it far easier to engage volunteer energy and expertise in community projects that matter to both the volunteer and the community at large.

Noting that all communities have an abundance of both talent and needs, Joe developed an innovative software program called "GroundCrew," which can instantly match those with available time and energy to projects that need volunteers—activities like tutoring, clearing trails, documenting local history, and helping seniors. Berkeley, California is now using GroundCrew to orchestrate a variety of community improvement projects.

Joe doesn't have money or marketing expertise. He does have persistence, vision, and a tested software product. This combination of passion and product has attracted the other elements he needed: talented senior administrators and investors with vision and drive. Together, they are building a social process that becomes "a powerful engine for local economies, local engagement, and local fun." For a look into a new way to play in the world, **visit www.groundcrew.us**.

What is your particular idea for what your community needs, or the world? What is your particular talent? Whom do you want and need on your team? Who else is engaged in the work you care about? What existing team or organization might you want to join?

Not everyone's talent is to have the big vision, to be able to craft the strategy to implement it. You may find your niche in simply having the original idea and the energy to keep it front and center until you attract allies with the requisite skills to make it happen. You may be a loyal supporter of a cause that is compelling, with money, advice, and feedback, or as a wise sounding board. Find a way to complement the visionary leaders with whom you want to be associated by offering the skills and connections they need but do not have. Find your fulfillment as a loyal team member eager to empower an important cause. Enjoy being part of a group that shares your own interests and passions. Be fearless about allying with others who love to do the things that dovetail with your own talents. Together we can!

ADDITIONAL RESOURCES YOU MAY ENJOY

Visit **www.meetup.com** where you can "do something, learn something, share something, change something."

CHAPTER 28

Create Space for the New

"No one ever got muscle by watching me lift weights."
—*Arnold Schwartzenegger*

MY FRIEND JUDY, of whom I spoke earlier, was stepping into her calling as a nutrition and energy healer at age 50. All of her earlier life paths, experiences, training, and true gifts seemed to converge in a newfound passion to offer this healing service to eager clients and friends.

She said "yes" to her "calling" not knowing the form her practice might take, nor even how it might manifest as a livelihood for her. Nevertheless, she leaned into it and trusted her sense that she was in the place she was meant to be, doing what she was meant to do. Metaphorically, she started lifting her own weights. She created space for her newly envisioned life in a variety of ways:

- **She created space in her schedule**
  Judy negotiated her employment schedule down from 5 days to 4, so that she would have time to start her new practice. To paraphrase a line from Field of Dreams: If you create an empty space, it will fill.

- **She created space to speak about what she loved**
  Judy identified a group of friends to convene one night a month in order to begin talking to others about her burgeoning skills and knowledge. This setting allowed her to promote dialogue, invite questions, and exercise her emerging clarity about her practice.

- **She created space on the Internet**
  For Judy, this meant creating a website to serve as an extended business

card. At first, she agonized about the project, fearing it would not be perfect. Perfection is one of the enemies of moving forward. With a suggestion that she simply start writing, Judy slowly gave herself permission to be messy and incoherent. After all, every website appropriately evolves in content and format. After a weekend devoted to "the start," Judy very quickly created a beautiful first-draft website, which she made available to friends and associates for feedback. The format evolved for another six months, and her newly available space started to fill as she became able to share what was important to her. To see her website today, **visit www.powerctr.com**.

- **She created internal space for an as-yet-unrealized dream.**
  Judy practiced daily meditation and energy exercises to keep her spirits strong and her good ideas flowing. She became energized around her intentions, even though, at the start, they were in the realm of the invisible.

It's important for you to create time and space for yourself on a regular basis. Do not fear temporary emptiness, or blank pages on your website or a clean desk, or a closet relieved of the unwearables. Don't avoid trips to the dump. One thing about empty spaces—their very existence seems to send a message that you are ready for something new to arrive.

This also means reminding yourself of your intentions, talking to your objections, and continuing to reframe the way you view yourself in the world. Here are a few reminders.

1. If what you are wanting is new and fearsome, keep asking the original questions: What do I love? What am I good at? How will I serve? Old beliefs don't dissolve in days, and will require some massaging, some confronting, some challenging, and some upgrading.

    For instance: *Today I am "good enough," and I demonstrate that by sitting down with a cup of tea and gazing out the window.*

2. Continue to play with your intention and affirm its presence in you or in the world. Be open to flow.

   For instance: *This is what I am wanting.... and this is how I envision it in its full manifestation.... The help I am looking for is looking for me also.*

3. Continue to identify and shift the powerful energetic scripts of childhood whenever you feel temporarily stuck.

4. Keep raising the question, "Is there anything else that might be holding me back?"

5. Ask frequently: "How else might I open space, or create space to accommodate the new? What in my current life needs to move out?"

ADDITIONAL RESOURCES YOU MAY ENJOY

Eat, Pray and Love: One Woman's Search for Everything—Across Italy, India and Indonesia by Elizabeth Gilbert, 2006. The author of this bestseller consciously created a year of space to allow her wounds to heal and the next phase of her life to take shape.

One Minute for Myself by Spencer Johnson, MD (co-author of the One Minute Manager), 1985.

Simple Abundance: A Daybook of Comfort and Joy by Sarah Ban Breathnach, 1995.

CHAPTER 29

❧

Make a Public Commitment

*"You cannot make yourself feel something you do not feel,
but you can make yourself do right in spite of your feelings."*
—Pearl S. Buck

IN A WORLD WHERE SYSTEMS—education, financial, economic, social, environmental—are breaking down, where corporate greed seems to be in overdrive, young and old are beginning to wonder: Will our grandchildren really have clean air and water and the energy they need to survive? How will the poorest of the poor be fed? Have we lost our way? Will corporate interests ever embrace multiple bottom lines and stand for the common good? Will we ever share the values which are consistent with our needs as an interdependent world wide community? Young people in MBA schools seem to be getting on the case—at least in terms of being willing to break with the past in public ways.

On June 5, 2009, twenty percent of the graduates of Harvard's 2009 MBA program were "feeling sufficiently distressed" about the current economic situation to publicly commit to carving a new path for themselves. Citing the mismanagement and single-mindedness of a generation of highly educated Wall Street MBAs, these students developed and signed an ethics pledge and challenged their fellow graduates from other institutions across the nation to follow suit.

Since that time, the MBA Oath project has grown exponentially. In a student-generated project, every major MBA school has been invited to set up an MBA Oath chapter on campus. Young people want to be proud of their profession of choice.

Without including the entire oath, I have extracted the particular commitments that brought tears to my eyes and hope to my heart.

From the preamble:

...I recognize my decisions can have far-reaching consequences that affect the well-being of individuals inside and outside my enterprise, today and in the future. As I reconcile the interests of different constituencies, I will face choices that are not easy for me and others....

From the promises:

- **I will** manage my enterprise in good faith, guarding against decisions and behavior that advance my own narrow ambitions but harm the enterprise and the societies it serves.
- **I will** take responsibility for my actions, and I will represent the performance and risks of my enterprise accurately and honestly.
- **I will** develop both myself and other managers under my supervision so that the profession continues to grow and contribute to the well-being of society.
- **I will** strive to create sustainable economic, social, and environmental prosperity worldwide.

Reading those promises, I feel hopeful. My sense is that those who are driven to discuss these issues with their colleagues, make commitments to their peers, and take an oath in the larger public realm and with future employers might be giving themselves an extra ethical undergirding for their professional decision-making. They might be energized to make a real difference in the world—more so than those who neither actively engaged in discussions nor put themselves "on record."

The MBA Oath Project is ripe for a long-term study—if anyone is interested. We don't know today how this public commitment, as expressed in a public oath, will move these young people along their career paths. We don't know if they really understand the breadth and depth of what their commitment entails. We don't know the impact of a group commitment. We don't know what signers will have contributed in 30 years, or how they will have changed the world, compared to the non-signers. But we do know intuitively that young people are really ready for a change and that deeply held values matter. I would state with some certainty that public commitments, grounded in deeply held values, matter even more.

While I just exhibited my enthusiasm for an example which is a large-scale national movement among MBA students, let's not overlook the importance of one's own individual public statement—perhaps yours. Showing yourself in public, as an individual, in terms of who you are and what you are about is a strategy not to be overlooked. As you contemplate what you want to do, the contribution you want to make, you, at the most basic personal level, can reveal yourself. You are sure to receive some extra energy and support, and perhaps even attract those who will hold you accountable.

> I remember the days of having recently received a diagnosis of MS. I felt vulnerable, alone and scared. Against well-intentioned advice, over a period of months I would announce as part of my introduction in workshops I was leading, or classes that I attended, that I had received this diagnosis, and was seeking alternative approaches to healing my condition. I was amazed at the number of people who eagerly approached me privately to share helpful resources. I felt much less alone, and much more energized with the support and information that came my way. I was relieved that I had intuitively dared to publicize myself, my path, my hopes and my needs, despite advice to the contrary.

What's your situation? What are you needing to say to your family, your friends, in your workplace, about who you are, what you care about, and what you are wanting and needing? It takes only one committed voice to launch a movement.

ADDITIONAL RESOURCES YOU MAY ENJOY

For those who want to know about the origins of the original oath and the current project mission, **visit www.mbaoath.org**.

Five Minds for the Future by Howard Gardner, 2009. Originator of the groundbreaking theory of multiple intelligences, Gardner suggests that mastery of five critical mind sets are demanded for effectiveness in our fast paced world, among them the ethical mind.

Finding Your Voice: Learning to Lead...Anywhere You Want to Make a Difference by Larraine R. Matusak, 1997.

A Force of Ones: Reclaiming Individual Power in a Time of Teams, Work Groups and Other Crowds by Stanley Herman, 1994.

When Corporations Rule the World by David Korten, 1995. A prolific bestselling author, lecturer, and engaged citizen, Korten has worked hard his entire life to understand the institutional sources of human dysfunction, and to create a path to a New Economy. Visit his Weblog **www.davidkorten.org.**

CHAPTER 30

Find Your Own Way...

"Today, like every other day, we wake up empty
and frightened. Don't open the door to the study
and begin reading. Take down a musical instrument.

Let the beauty we love be what we do.
There are hundreds of ways to kneel and kiss the ground."

—Rumi

YES, THERE ARE MANY WAYS TO GET INTO ACTION, stay focused, have fun, and do good. The way that will work best for you is your own, unique way—enriched and informed by all that you can learn from others, and energized by your values and your moral compass.

I'm sure I have overlooked many other exciting and useful illustrations of ways to get into action. I welcome your comments, thoughts, stories as you make the changes and commitments that will carry you deeper into your own, unique path.

Let this book be the start of many conversations.

Visit www.whynotdowhatyoulove.com.

Reflection

You've gotten into action. Or you are still thinking about it...

How are you feeling?

— Get a cup or tea or coffee, find a quiet spot, sit down.

— Appreciate that there is nothing to do right now.

— Take a long slow deep breath, and take your pulse:

We're taking a break for some reflection.

• What concerns arise for you?

• What questions arise for you?

• What examples most resonate as being relevant for you and your next steps right now?

And most important...

What's becoming clear to you?

PART SIX

Take Time for Reflection—Always

TAKE TIME FOR REFLECTION—ALWAYS

THE TIME TO REFLECT IS ALWAYS. So here we are in Part Six, offering a chapter that may have more meaning to you six months from now—or even six years from now. If you have followed the suggestions in this book, you have set the intentions you have set, and you have taken the actions you have taken. You will have gotten some results—which may be more of what you love, or a piece of your calling that will continue to build on itself. Whatever happens, you get to learn from it. It's amazing how many people tell me, when looking back at their lives, "So that's why I was called to that piece of work. It was essential in bringing me where I am now!"

Contemplation is the highest form of activity.

— ARISTOTLE —

Being accountable to yourself happens in the times you set aside to pause and reflect. It happens when you purposefully and consciously address some basic questions:

- How am I doing?

- How am I doing with my efforts to stay true to my intentions?

- To what extent have I created more of what I love in life?

Today, or in six months, or in six years, it's good to review the commitments you made to yourself. Are you keeping them? Missing them? Changing them? Ready for a new phase in your life?

You may also want to revisit the questions from previous sections. The act of repeatedly asking and answering questions will help you remember what you love and what you are good at. It will also help you see those situations where you might be missing the mark.

184

If you keep finding reasons not to move forward, that's a signal that you may have ignored an important deep-seated wish, or may have neglected to identify a key belief barrier, or may have gotten only part-way to the truth about what you love. It's possible that your answers are still mixed with information that came from others—rather than drawing on your deepest feelings, needs, and wants.

Conversely, you may be on exactly the right path, and parts of the puzzle pieces to your ultimate destiny are being put in place—piece by piece without your awareness. Life may even offer you a few more detours so that you can pick up some necessary puzzle pieces temporarily missing. There is no failure on this journey. There is only staying true to yourself, accepting the callings of the moment, which are likely to be the building blocks to a larger calling. (And yes, 20 years later, the book I thought I "should" write way back then is what you hold in your hands today. Timing is everything.)

Don't blame yourself; sometimes life signals that it is time to stop, rest, and regroup. When that happens, it is good to listen; stop, rest, and regroup. Ultimately, go back to the drawing board. You may go through several years of life experiments in order to uncover what you are meant to do. From each of those experiments, or way stations, you will learn what is fulfilling and what is not. They will be part of the picture. And you will take a next step and the next. In retrospect, you'll find that the timing always makes sense. As you discover more and more of the meaning of your path, your life will begin to move in flow; excuses will fall away. That's the way calling works.

Most importantly, consider the Accountability Questions listed above as a gentle bonus: they are not an invitation to blame or beat yourself up. Use these questions, and revisit the earlier questions. Check in with yourself. I repeat: Be gentle. Enjoy the continuing process of self-discovery which is life.

The following chapters show others reflecting on their lives from different angles and different perspectives. As you read their stories, see what light you can shine on your own desire to be accountable to yourself on this journey.

CHAPTER 31

❧

Being Accountable

"For most people, change means keeping things the same, only better."
—*Tom Fosse*

IF YOU ARE ONE OF THOSE who is already living their soul purpose, their deep destiny, or their purpose in life, then you probably don't think about it much. You are frequently in flow, responding to whatever shows up on a daily basis. That is who you are. That is the way you are allowing things to happen for you.

However, if you are still struggling to get the results you desire, you may want to check in with yourself. You may want to revisit the all-important alignment query: Why might I be unwilling? No blame allowed, just inquiry.

A friend of mine wrote a long manuscript, an initial draft of a book he intended to write about something important to him at the time. It lay dormant for quite a while. When we next spoke, perhaps a year later, he reported: "I've asked myself why I have not been willing to keep going with this book—why I have not been accountable to my initial intention. Here's the thing, Martha. It's not exactly the book I really want to write. I want to write about my journey through life, some of which is in that manuscript, but it's not focused in the way I'd like."

Perfect. His effort was not wasted. The truth came out. If you keep asking the questions, the true direction emerges in its own time.

Strategies for personal accountability are as varied as individual styles:

* Some people will create checklists, and deadlines, and calendars—and hopefully will be gentle with themselves when they miss a mark.

- Some will benefit from a discipline of naming three successes a day. If at first it is hard, it will become easier and more enjoyable with practice. And it will show you how far you are moving and whether you are moving towards your deepest desires.

- Others will set up a support system of friends, or a regular meeting with a helper, to whom they will verbalize their intentions and enlist the encouragement needed to keep up their pace.

- One very formal way of using the support of friends is to set up what is known as a Clearness Committee, a process which originated with the Quakers. The committee is made up of people who care about you, who will listen to your ramblings, and who will ask questions to help clarify what's troubling you and what you might want to do about it. Important to note: Clearness Committee members are trained to ask open-ended, strategic questions only; they give no advice, and have no agenda other than to elicit the seeker's own clarity. (See Appendix A for more information.)

- Some may also set up time for personal reflection on a daily basis, akin to cleaning the sink, meditation, yoga, a daily walk in nature, journal writing.

- And some will make a calendar appointment with themselves to review the Accountability Questions in order to determine how they are doing and what they may want to recalibrate.

- Others will actively experiment with what's emerging. So, for example, my friend who wants to sing more, but is fearful about engaging an audience, makes arrangements to sing at senior centers. She thus begins to do what she loves in public. Anything that keeps you moving on, doing more of what you love, is an act of accountability.

Accountability is a concept that tends to be serious in tone. When discovering and deepening one's calling and commitment, however, it's important to be able to play with it. Take your dreams seriously and yourself lightly. When responsibility and accountability come from deep and personal commitment, they tend to invite experimentation and play, rather than burdensome "should's." **Be intentionally responsible to yourself, with a light touch.**

By way of example, here are two women, **Bernice** and **Sally**, who were deeply serious about making changes in their lives. Each had concluded that if they did not allow themselves to give priority to their own needs, they would never be able to spend more of their time on what they loved—on what they wanted.

Bernice is a woman who by personality was a "caretaker." She typically put everyone else in her life first. This is a quality often appreciated by others, and Bernice was well-loved. She could always be counted on to help out. But her own needs, desires, and passions tended to be left out of her daily attentions. She was visibly fatigued. As part of her work around calling, Bernice used the accountability practice of "three successes": she began naming on a daily basis three ways she had managed to address her needs and to, perhaps, do a bit less for others. She knew this would be hard. Soon, however, she shared her progress report with lively enthusiasm: "I was so tired. I just bit the bullet and went to a potluck dinner and *I didn't take anything.*" For Bernice, this was a personal act of courage and a major milestone. She discovered that the world did not collapse when she took care of herself.

Sally on the other hand realized that her greatest barrier was her own timidity. She felt unable to step out and do what she knew in her gut was right for her, for fear that others wouldn't like it. After reflecting on this issue and facing directly the beliefs about herself that drove that fear, Sally created and proudly wore a new charm bracelet. Prominently hanging from the bracelet were six letters: **N M W A E T**. These were not the initials of her children: rather, she explained, this was her daily reminder to stay on track with *her* goals, **No Matter What Anyone Else Thinks.**

When I think of these two women, I still chuckle. With gentle determination, it is absolutely possible to stay accountable to yourself with laughter and a light touch.

CHAPTER 32

Am I Happy?

"If your compassion does not include yourself,
it is incomplete."
—*Jack Kornfield*

TOO MUCH OF A GOOD THING, even exactly what one may have wished for, may sneakily deteriorate into, well, just too much. For much of my life, I worked hard doing what I loved—often too hard, without breaks, and without balance. I deluded myself into thinking work and play would always be one and the same, and I considered my occasional exhausted collapses as simply the cycle of my life.

I was finally able to reflect on this phenomenon through someone else's experience: Mary Pipher's 2009 memoir, *Seeking Peace: Chronicles of the World's Worst Buddhist.*

After a rather chaotic and unique childhood, Mary ended up with a good education, a Ph.D in psychology, a solid marriage, and a professional calling as a family therapist. She was a self-described nurturer at core, loving her life as parent and wife and therapist. A near-obsessive seeker of interesting experiences and the truths of life, particularly in the areas of child development and the health of families, Mary maintained a busy and nourishing life for herself and those she loved. As her children grew and became more independent, she filled her newly freed time with another passion—writing. Starting with articles, she ultimately penned several books to such critical acclaim that they resided for months on best-seller lists. Her whole life was working.

But then there was that invitation to appear on Oprah! This brought further invitations to share her professional expertise with a wider audience—and it catapulted her into a new and very different life. The envy of her professional colleagues and friends, Mary began to travel the world, giving speeches and seminars.

However, lonely hotel rooms, other people's cooking, a routine of life on the road, on the plane, off the plane, began to take its toll. People in her profession wanted more of Mary than she was able to give. Beyond that, she missed her family. They missed her. Her life had lost its balance and its joy. Her body was rebelling, and Mary felt she had lost herself.

Acknowledging her internal disconnect and unhappiness, Mary stopped. Over time, she designed a serious rest and recovery program. It was clearly a challenge, but the "world's worst Buddhist," with the ever-active mind, learned how to "be." Her story ultimately ends well, and the lessons of her journey are valuable to her many readers.

"Am I happy?" As you begin following the paths of your calling, this is an important question to visit and revisit. Doing meaningful work, work that we love, can sometimes abscond with our lives.

"Now and then it's good to pause in our pursuit of happiness and just be happy."

— ANONYMOUS—

Regular reflection cannot guarantee happiness. But it can prompt a paying of attention—a new choosing, a getting back on track—which is essential to a life well-lived. You might want to keep a few questions handy in your back pocket. Such as, "Although I'm proud that I'm doing good work and having fun, what other important needs of mine are not being met?" And, "What is my body telling me about how healthy I really am?"

Finally, never forget to pose the question that is neither selfish nor insignificant, "Am I happy?"

CHAPTER 33

A Middle-Aged Mother Muses on Her Next Call to Calling

"For every promise you make to others, keep one to yourself."
—*Sarah Ban Breathnach*

SOME GIFTS AND TALENTS ARE WAITING in the background for the right time to express themselves. Other gifts and talents are seeking to be expressed in a new life role. If you find yourself at a stopping point in one area of your life, or a crossroads, or a decision point, what would be your strategy for reflection? How would you make time and space to pull together the threads of what seems to be calling to you?

Deb Belle was at that point. Her need to give full attention to parenting her four children was ending. Her need to give attention to the next steps in her calling journey was at hand. The way she entered reflection to hold her accountable to the next steps she needed to take in her life was to write about it.

On May 26, 2009, the journal entry Deb shared with a group of fellow writers really touched me. And so, what follows are the words she dared to let her heart speak on her path to calling clarity.

> THESE WORDS: encapsulate, ludicrous, especially, indistinguishable, are just words. But place them side by side in the right order and they form a story: This is ludicrous. To encapsulate this makes it especially indistinguishable.

Letters. Words. Place them vertically and you have a poem.

       Indistinguishable.
       Ludicrous.
       Encapsulate especially.

Writing. Crafting. Working.

No, not working. And since it is not work, I can't quantify my ability.

An electrician, carpenter, teacher, asked how long they have practiced their trade, can deliver an answer that will get an impressed nod of the head. They can even state their level of skill, specific skill.

But a writer:

       How long have you been writing?
       Publish anything?
       Make any money from that?

And the head just keeps a small, nodding movement as if to keep the brain and mouth disengaged so nothing rude comes out.

       So when are you getting a real job?
       That's a hobby. right?
       Anything?

God forbid you actually say you're good at it. You wouldn't expect to go to an accountant and have them say:

       Oh, I am not that good.
       I just play around with it now and then.
       Nah, just do it for my health.

I've worked at an underappreciated career for twenty-one years—mother, homemaker, family manager—why choose writing now…

I'm a writer. But, even saying it sounds a little audacious. Even while I'm trying to keep this frustrated little rant going, I'm thinking, "You know, I think I'm done with the ranting. I'm a writer and it feels good. And yeah, I am good at it."

And why do I find it necessary to even write this down? There are lots of books on writing and about writing. And they are great: Anne Lamott's Bird by Bird, Stephen King's On Writing, Natalie Golberg's Writing down the Bones, and on and on.

I thought I could read them and find the secret formula. All I found is there isn't one. In fact, I berated myself for twenty one plus years because I wasn't following the rules—early morning, two hours, after a walk, ten pages a day, by hand, in, away, from, late…

There is no formula.

I scratched something here and there and shoved it away. Pulled it out. Added a page or two.

Then a day came when I shared a couple of poems and the response was, "Got any more like this? Sounds like a journey."

That is what writing is. Just recording a journey, maybe not the details of who you are or what you're doing, but a journey of where your mind, body and spirit travel.

So, that's why I'm writing all this down: because I'm getting to this place where I see the words I've connected—and realize—

I'm a writer.

In August of 2009, Deb Belle was accepted into the MFA (Master of Fine Arts in Writing) program at Spalding University.

Yes, paths shift. There are endings and there are new beginnings throughout our lives. Unanticipated detours surprise us. It is perhaps only in hindsight that we can fathom the deep ways in which everything in our life connects, and how constant has been the unique "calling" at the core of our lives. In the meantime, as we are being refined and polished by life, be patient with the confusions during change, accept the times of not knowing, and seek solace in the questions to which answers will come.

CHAPTER 34

❧

Get a Life!

"People have it wrong when they say: 'If only I were healthy, I would be happy.' It's the reverse we have some control over, 'If only I were happy, I would be healthy.'"
—*Zoran Hochstätter*

SOURCES OF REFLECTION COME FROM MANY PLACES. Now that you have reached the end of this book, perhaps these words from a graduation speech, "Get a Life!" by Pulitzer Prize winner Anna Quindlen*, will resonate. As you continue to gather your thoughts about the place you wish to occupy and the calling that is calling you, it is words like these that help to keep life and work in perspective.

YOU CANNOT BE REALLY FIRST RATE AT YOUR WORK if your work is all you are. So here's what I wanted to tell you today:

Get a life. A real life, not a manic pursuit of the next promotion, the bigger pay cheque, the larger house. Do you think you'd care so very much about those things if you blew an aneurysm one afternoon or found a lump in your breast?

Get a life in which you notice the smell of salt water pushing itself on a breeze at the seaside, a life in which you stop and watch how a red-tailed hawk circles over the water, or the way a baby scowls with concentration when she tries to pick up a sweet with her thumb and first finger.

Get a life in which you are not alone. Find people you love, and who love you. And remember that love is not leisure, it is work. Pick up the phone. Send an email. Write a letter. Get a life in which you are generous. And realize that life is the best thing ever, and that you have no business taking it for granted. Care so deeply about its goodness that you want to spread it around. Take money you would have spent on beer and give it to charity. Work in a soup kitchen. Be a big brother or sister. All of you want to do well. But if you do not do good too, then doing well will never be enough.

.... It is so easy to waste our lives, our days, our hours, and our minutes. It is so easy to take for granted the color of our kids' eyes, the way the melody in a symphony rises and falls and disappears and rises again. It is so easy to exist instead of to live.

....Learn to be happy. And think of life as a terminal illness, because if you do, you will live it with joy and passion as it ought to be lived.

* *Anna Quindlen, mother of 3, prolific author, columnist, and very wise woman, has long been a popular graduation speaker. I regret that the actual source and date of the speech from which these excerpts are taken are not definitive. To enjoy more of her wisdom, and the additional sources of reflection they provide, seek her out on the Internet and in her many books.*

EPILOGUE

DURING THIS YEAR AND THIS PROCESS of putting pen to paper about what matters to me, I'm finding I've become more clear in three areas.

First, I have come to more fully appreciate the life I've lived doing what I have loved. I've felt privileged to have been a Peace Corps volunteer, a public school teacher, a National Park Ranger, a founding principal of my own management consulting and training practice, and a leader coach (**30 of those professional years as Martha Spice**).

Second, it has been a healing journey to bring to life my belief that doing more of what we love is good for us and good for those others with whom we share the planet. This book you're holding in your hand is a personal milestone for me. Having arrived at this milestone, I'm newly aware that I've had too much fun to stop here. Therefore, I'm assuring that the title question will continue to live through its own website **www.whynotdowhatyoulove.com**.

> To find our calling is to find the intersection of our deep passion and the world's deep hunger.
>
> — FREDERICK BUECHNER

Third, I've gotten clearer that we are sitting in "very interesting times" in the span of planetary history. Now retired, back in my childhood home, having reclaimed my maiden name, I've had the space and the inclination to sit with broader questions as our country changes before my eyes. An old order seems to be crumbling. Where there are cracks, there are openings for the new. The world seems to be inviting us to "wake up" and take notice. The "new" will be influenced by the seeds we plant in the emerging crevices and the sprouts we choose to nourish. The world is really, really, awaiting our gifts.

In this moment, I believe there is some urgency. We seem to have arrived at a tipping point where our choices matter more than ever. We can choose to either contaminate our future livelihoods, or tend to each other and to the earth in a way that sustains us. We have an opportunity to reclaim the power of love, justice, and community.

Don't be concerned if you still have questions about the role you want to play on this earth at this time! I do believe that questions are more potent than answers. Good questions, held in the psyche, seem to answer themselves after a while. With good questions, you are in safe company. Just be sure to hold onto the notion that daring to use yourself well is an act of courage of which you are capable. The answers will come when you are ready for them.

Please visit the website to see what will next emerge from this 70-year-old and her new community of friends. At the very least, the dot.com site will be a place where you can contribute stories about your journey and learn about the choices others are making.

Finally, I am so grateful to all those who have found this book helpful, those who will share it with others, and those will who take the time to be in touch. The heartfelt wishes I extend to all will not surprise you: this is a time to honor your aspirations and your talents and to think about how they can matter to all on the planet.

I wish for you the happiness and well-being that comes from choosing to join the expanding tribe of the courageous, the fulfilled, and the useful, knowing your unique gifts are making a difference in a world which needs all our talents.

Martha Johnson
January, 2010

BE IN TOUCH!

www.whynotdowhatyoulove.com

www.linkedin.com/in/whynotdowhatyoulove

www.taketimeforyou.net

APPENDIX

More Resources
For You

APPENDIX A

If you want more good books and authors...

Many of the chapters are already followed by 1 or 2 or 5 additional chapter-relevant resources I thought the reader might find interesting. In Appendix A, I am choosing to highlight authors, many prolific, who have been constant over the years writing and thinking about familiar topics: life purpose and patterns, skills, strengths and talents, life work, doing what you were meant to do, making life changes on your own and with group support. They have their own style and approach and perspective. Don't hesitate to seek out their many published books beyond what I have listed here. Some focus on philosophy, some on specific tools, and some on a combination.

A Hidden Wholeness: The Journey Toward an Undivided Life by Parker Palmer, 2009. In the latest of his many books, Palmer discusses how to set up and facilitate "circles of trust," ways for people to explore themselves, their lives, and their moral compass with the support of a safe and supportive community of explorers.

The Clearness Committee: A Communal Approach to Discernment by Parker Palmer, **www.wildacresleadership.org/pdf/clearness_committee.pdf**

I made special mention of 'the Clearness Committee' in chapter 31 as one of the ways to get support for one's clarity. The concept, originating with the Quakers in the 1660s, has been promulgated by Parker Palmer in many of his writings. His 4-page article is a good introduction and accessible through the link above.

Within the Religious Society of Friends, the clearness committee represents a process for gaining clarity on a concern or a dilemma. As Palmer states in his article, the Clearness Committee is testimony to the fact that there are no external authorities on life's deepest issues, not clergy or therapists or scholars; there is only the authority that lies within each of us waiting to be heard. I would add that vital life issues such as decisions around calling and contribution are ripe for this process, providing it is properly used by those who are experienced with the specific method recommended.

The Center for Courage and Renewal has a mission to reconnect who you are with what you do. It is where Circle of Trust retreats are offered by Parker Palmer and a staff of skilled facilitators. Solitude, reflection and deep listening are encouraged. See website for schedule of events **www.couragerenewal.org**.

Do What You Love, the Money Will Follow by Marsha Sinetar, 1989. This is Sinetar's still popular classic.

Elegant Choices, Healing Choices by Marsha Sinetar, 1988.
And many more...

Wishcraft: How to Get What You Really Want Barbara Sher and Annie Gottlieb, 2003

I Could Do Anything If I Only Knew What It Was: How to Discover What You Really Want and How to Get It by Barbara Sher, 1995.
And many more...

Care of the Soul: A Guide for Cultivating Depth and Sacredness in Everyday Life by Thomas Moore, 1994 and *A Life at Work: The Joy of Discovering What You Were Born to Do*, 2009. And many more...

Composing a Life by Mary Catherine Bateson, 1990

What Color is Your Parachute? by Richard Nelson Bolles. A classic, originally published in 1970, Bolles has made it an updated annual and has authored or co-authored many additional books, including his latest: *The Job-Hunters' Survival Guide: How to Find Hope and Rewarding Work, Even When There Are No Jobs.* And many more...

The Soul's Code: In Search of Character and Calling by James Hillman, 1997. And many more...

Go Put Your Strengths to Work: 6 Powerful Steps to Achieve Outstanding Performance by Marcus Buckingham, 2007. And many more.

And for variety...

The Renaissance Soul: Life Design for People with Too Many Passions to Pick Just One by Margaret Lobenstine, 2006

Deep Type: A powerful New Way to Determine Personality Type and Deeper Type Analysis by Alan Gilburg, 2006

Callings: Finding and Following an Authentic Life by Gregg Levoy, 1997

The Anti-Resume Revolution: The Innovative and Forward-Thinking Guide for Job Seekers and Aspiring Entrepreneurs Who Want to do What They Love by Angela Lussier, 2009. A no-nonsense and refreshingly personal guide to putting yourself out there in order to do what you love in the world. **Visit www.my365degrees.com**.

APPENDIX B

If you want to learn more about Affirmations...

I mentioned the use of "affirmations" several times as a powerful tool for change and new life design. **Here are two books** which demonstrate the process in different ways and give many examples which will be useful.

Words that Heal by Douglas Bloch, 1988. "What you say is what you get" is the process Bloch describes briefly. He then offers key affirmation statements on which to meditate for different issues in your life.

Five Wishes by Gay Hendricks, 2009. Challenged by one powerful question from a teacher at mid-life, Gay shares how he created a successful and fulfilling personal and professional life with affirmative clarity. Here are two personal examples which provide further illustration.

1. **Everyone can experiment by reconstructing their belief about "time."**
    We all verbalize our relationship with time; usually that we never have enough. This is such a common construct; it comes up with clients frequently, and we don't think to question it as "our" construct. Those I invite to make a change in their relationship to time generally report a successful experience reducing stress and angst. One example I cherish is that of my mother, who I heard one day complaining vociferously that she didn't have enough time. Here's the story:

    Mom was visiting me in Maryland, complaining that in her retired life, she had no time. I was surprised as when she was working and raising 6 children, I had never recalled this complaint. Always active, always busy, always practical, she was getting older and apparently feeling the stress of so much she still wanted to do and not enough time to do it.

I quickly shared with my mother, then 70, the simple technology of selecting a more useful truth on which to operate her life. "Yes," I said, "you believe you have no time. But, a more useful idea is that you have all the time there is—24 hours a day." I wrote down one basic phrase on a card and asked her to repeat it daily, sitting down, taking deep breaths, particularly in moments when she was feeling stressed: "I have all the time I need to do what I want to do."

Very skeptical, my staunch New England mother, who cringed at "lying" to herself, wondered out loud how I ever made a living writing phrases down on cards for people. But she decided she had nothing to lose by experimenting and agreed to try it out.

She left for her home in Massachusetts and I heard from her about six weeks later. It was an amazing call, first because she actually called long distance, which her Depression Era upbringing tended to prevent her from doing except in emergencies. Second, because my very skeptical and very practical mother had only called to report how pleased she was with her program. She was feeling relaxed and happy and had plenty of time to carry on with her life. She thanked me profusely.

Although the belief about having no time may be a more surface excuse that masks other more immobilizing objections, it is a popular one. I have watched many people make a major life-enhancing change from seeing 24 hours as "not enough" to seeing 24 hours as "enough." How we see it is, after all, our choice. And the latter way of seeing it, it seems to me, is more useful for moving forward with ease.

2. **Sometimes it takes creativity and the use of paradox to craft an affirmation that will really penetrate one's rigid and long-held beliefs about oneself.**

In the early days of learning about affirmations, I was struggling. I kept coming up against what I saw as a core, debilitating, belief which was affecting everything in my life: I am not good enough. Here's my story:

I tried going after it directly by stating its direct opposite: "I am good enough." That was too big of a leap for me at the time and I couldn't really entertain the new idea no matter how much I wanted it to be true in my life.

Feeling frustrated, I wrote to Leonard Orr, one of my teachers at the time, and an originator of this process. I asked him how to neutralize my lifelong childhood belief that "I am not good enough." A genius at bollixing deeply embedded belief systems with an indirect approach, he sent back my prescription: "I, Martha, am not good enough to invalidate my own Divinity." I laughed and laughed and cried and laughed. The crafting of the statement bypassed all my previous objections, cooperated with my original premise, while completely turning it on its head. The process of neutralizing an old idea had started.

[While I hesitate to claim that deeply held very core beliefs ever entirely go away, I *will* claim that with awareness, with help, and with some positive self-programming, the power they have to hold us back can be significantly diminished. A little persistance and creativity go a long way.]

Leonard Orr's earlier books from the 1970s and those of his colleagues Sondra Ray and Bob Mandell, may now be out of print. If you find them in a second-hand bookstore, they are worth a look.

APPENDIX C

If you want to know more about therapeutic modalities that support your health and therefore your ability to make changes in your life:

It probably doesn't need saying, but I'll say it anyway. *In order to be effective in life, your health is critical, meaning the health of your body, mind, and spirit.* So, I highlight below for your own research, some of the more innovative and supportive complementary therapies which are growing in use and popularity. Because my personal experience with them has been positive, I feel comfortable sharing the list that this Appendix C contains.

The energy modalities are safe and gentle. They can be useful in dissolving fears and beliefs that stand in the way of you being able to call forth the personal passions and contributions which most seek expression in your life. They promote health and wellbeing. Best of all they can be easily explored in books, tapes, free newsletters, and workshops, that teach the self-application basics. Although this list is not exhaustive, perhaps it will lead you to entertain some different ways of dealing with whatever you identify that may be holding you back from pursuing your dreams.

Emotional Freedom Technique (EFT) **www.eftforums.com**

Tapas Acupressure Techniques (TAT) **www. tatlife.com**

Donna Eden's Energy Medicine **www.innersource.net**

David Feinstein's Energy Psychology **www.innersource.net**

Psych-K **www.psych-k.com**

Energy therapies are increasingly and succssfully being applied to help returning veterans relieve combat trauma and reclaim satisfying lives. One of many such projects is sponsored by the **Soul Medicine Institute**. Visit **www.stressproject.org.**

The Domančić Method **www.healingbioenergy.com**
This protocol was created 35 years ago by Zdenko Domančić, who still serves patients world-wide in his clinic in Slovenia. Since 2008, this protocol is being introduced in the United States by cinematographer and Domančić Method trainer, Zoran Hochstätter. I suspect it will grow in reach and reputation quite quickly.

Related Books:

Molecules of Emotion: The Science Behind Mind-Body Medicine by Candace Pert, PhD., 1997.

The Biology of Belief: Unleashing the Power of Consciousness, Matter, and Miracles by Bruce Lipton, PhD., 2005

The Genie in Your Genes: Epigenetic Medicine and the New Biology of Intention by Dawson Church, PhD., 2008. An expansive, empowering and understandable introduction to the field of Energy Medicine. Includes 300 scientific studies and ways you can take control of your health, wellbeing and future.

Soul Medicine: Awakening Your Inner Blueprint for Abundant Health and Energy by Dawson Church, PhD. and Norman Shealy, Md., PhD, 2008

Authentic Happiness: Using the New Positiive Psychology to Realize Your Potential for Lasting Fulfillment by Martin E.P. Seligman, 2003

Mind, Medicine, and Miracles: Lessons Learned about Self-Healing from a Surgeon's Experience with Exceptional Patients by Bernie Siegal, MD., 1990.

Energy Medicine: Balance Your Body's Energies for Optimal Health, Joy, and Vitality by Donna Eden, 2008

Soul Retrieval: Mending the Fragmented Self by Sandra Ingerman, 1991

Who would you be without your story? Dialogues with Byron Katie by Carol Williams, Editor, 2008

A Short Guide to a Happy Life, 2000 and *Being Perfect* by Anna Quindlen, 2005. And many more...

A few more references...

In the spirit of full disclosure, I, Martha, have been living for 13 years challenged by a chronic illness—multiple sclerosis. Therefore I am aware of how inextricably linked are vibrant health and being able to do in the world what we aspire to do.

Part Four of this volume focuses on identifying and relieving us of beliefs which are toxic to moving forward towards our dreams. The energy therapies referenced above are highly effective in collapsing those negative scripts. Immediately prior to book printing, I realized that I would regret not having mentioned at least a few of the additional supportive resources and references which address the health of our bodies. The full story is that we must heal our minds AND treat our bodies with respect. The two are connected. Detoxing both of them help to maintain our natural and deserved vitality and clear the path to finding our true calling.

Clearspring Health Center in Arkansas
Dr. Michael Broeg has developed innovative natural health programs built around systemic detoxification and deep tissue restoration. These processes help normalize body functions so the body can begin to heal itself.
Visit: www.clearspringshealth.com.

Kangen Water™ from Enagic

In my experience, drinking alkaline ionized Kangen Water™ from Enagic, certified as a medical device in Japan, empowers all of the above mentioned protocols. It also detoxifies the body and builds the energy and healing necessary to one's total well being. Be warned: Internet chatter can be confusing to people seeking trustworthy information about this water system. Feel free to email **info@whynotdowhatyoulove.com**.

The Enzyme Factor by Dr Hiromi Shinya. M.D., 2007

The pH Miracle: Balance Your Diet, Reclaim Your Health by Robert Young, PhD. and Shelley Redford Young, 2003

Detoxify or Die by Sherry A. Rogers, MD, 2002. This author has specialized in what is now called environmental medicine—how we get sick from what's around us, and how we can detoxify.

Unexpected Recoveries: Seven Steps to Healing Body, Mind, and Soul, when Serious Illness Strikes by Tom Monte, 2005. Tom is a life and health counselor based in Amherst, Massachusetts. He is a best selling writer of a multitude of health-related books and co-author of *Taking Woodstock*.

Fortunately, all of the innovative and supportive therapies mentioned throughout Appendix C are beginning to attract the research they deserve.

The usual disclaimer applies: *The list of energy therapies and resources for health represent the author's recommendations from her own personal experience. They are included here solely for informational purposes and are not intended as a substitute for advice from your physician or other health care professional.*

APPENDIX D

If you want to check out an expert practitioner...

Experienced practitioners abound in most communities. They have sought advanced training and certification in a variety of energy modalities and utilize them as a primary or adjunct modality in their healing practices. There are many reasons you may decide that you want to seek a qualified counselor or practitioner:

- With some issues, it may be hard to wear two hats at the same time, that of self-practitioner and client. An objective witness will often be able to listen to your issues and help you find the most useful wording for your specific need.

- The issue or trauma which you are trying to neutralize is too big for you to handle with basic knowledge.

- You are using the protocol, but it does not seem to be having the desired result.

- You know there is a problem, but you just don't know where to begin.

Below I mention three individuals local to me in Western Massachusetts, with whose work I am familiar. They are all practitioners experienced in helping clients neutralize disabling beliefs and fears that block fulfillment and life satisfaction, such as the ones we have discussed in this book. They work in person and by phone. I include them so you can have a look at how a few practitioners with different skills and interests describe themselves.

One has a special expertise in the personal alignment approaches suggested in Part Four of this book in addition to other trainings and certifications. Two have special expertise and certifications the newer energy modalities as well as other protocols. All are doing what they are love to do and have taken this journey themselves. By visiting their websites, you can learn more about the healing practice each has been been "called" to do.

If you want help with the process I called the "big nudge," generally described in Part Four of this book, I'm happy to recommend:

Joseph DiCenso

www.joseph-dicenso.com

A personal and organizational consultant, a counselor and facilitator of change, Joseph's mantra has long been: "Bring more of yourself to life!"

Be on the lookout for Joseph's book-in-process! The working title is *Courageous Living: Make a Better World by Living the Life You Long For*.

If you want to experience how an energy protocol can neutralize and release blocks and barriers, I'm happy to recommend:

Stefan Gonick

www.stefangonick.com

A Gestalt trained therapist, Stefan specializes in the use of Emotional Freedom Techniques, commonly referred to as "EFT-Tapping."

Judy Grupenhoff, MS

www.powerctr.com

Judy is a nutritionist, trained in Hawaiian energy healing protocols and a certified Tapas Accupressure Techniques (TAT) Professional.

ACKNOWLEDGEMENTS

I AM GRATEFUL FOR THE SUPPORT of family, friends and to all those whose stories I have shared.

I want to credit my parents who allowed me to do whatever I felt "called" to do in the early days of leaving the nest. I remember my father being incredulous about my going into the Peace Corps, in 1963, still a new and untested endeavor. He asked one question: "Why would you want to go and dig ditches?" Nevertheless, no one kept me from applying for probably the most important experience of my lifetime, and there was no ditch-digging involved. My parents' support, were they alive today, would have extended to this book, even though for their "duty bound" generation the ideas would have been a bit radical.

I want to acknowledge my editor, Kathy Dunn, who lovingly understood my message and massaged my prose so that the ideas might reach those who are hungry for them. And the members of the Main Street Writer's group, who listened to my initial written ramblings about this topic and told me they expected signed copies.

I appreciate my subscription to Karen Jandorf's daily quote offerings, Season of Non-Violence, many of which found their way into this book. My suspicion is that her calling is to supply inspiration to herself and others, highlighting the past and present wisdom from every corner of the world.

I credit and enjoy life's great synchronicities. One of these was Judy Grupenhoff's arrival as my project was being initiated and her new calling was making itself known. We supported each other, gave each other feedback and edited for each other. Being able to bounce ideas off another person who spoke my language helped this book along significantly.

And finally, with an honesty tinged with regret, I must acknowledge the gift of a chronic illness which gives me time to slow down and write, and keeps me focused on the things I can do at home. Without that particular "gift," I'd probably be on a treadmill in pursuit of something, trying to deny an aging process which truly does bring its own special rewards.

ABOUT THE COVER

YOU HOLD IN YOUR HAND A BOOK that is imbued with calling energy—from cover to cover. First, the book "called" to be written, and I felt "called" to be the cooperating scribe. Second, the theme of "calling" brought forth the photographs as well.

Photos of the meadow on Pearl Street, behind the author's home, at the base of the Mt. Holyoke Range, were generously contributed by **Harry Lavo**. A talented and successful corporate executive during his prime career years, he was delighted to give his real passions more priority in retirement.

The two chairs on the front cover are placed in a special section of the meadow—a labyrinth—which was "called" into being by **Judy Grupenhoff** as she stepped into her work as an energy healer. A labyrinth is an ancient pattern for walking meditation; it is designed to promote life clarity. Within a 3-week period, everything that was needed to design and lay out the labyrinth was easily acquired, or miraculously discovered.

This cover photo also acknowledges the later-in-life passions and contributions of my father, **Richard L. Johnson**, and my brother, **Peter R. Johnson**. Both men dedicated themselves to conserving beautiful places in perpetuity, in the areas surrounding the Mt. Holyoke Range, and on Cape Cod. I am pleased and proud that father and brother honored their own callings—one of the results of which is that my meadow is forever protected under the Forest Legacy conservation easement program and can never be developed.

May the energy that this book carries assist you in all the ways you desire.

What's Next?

MY HOPE is that this book will inspire others like it.

The chronicle you have just read centers predominantly around ordinary people I knew or noticed in Western Massachusetts who do what they love. It would have taken many more books to fully capture all the inspirational stories that exist just in my area. I therefore invite bloggers, writers, observers, wherever you reside, to join the cause. Continue to make the case with your own local and regional stories of the heretofore unheralded: Doing what one loves and making a difference, really matters to the health and well being of us all.

I also hope that there will be a sequel. I'd love to see captured, in a more focused way, the proliferation of passions which are being applied to local, and regional efforts to sustain our existence on the planet. I can even imagine a title for whomever might have the passion to write such a sequel. **Why Not Do What You Love and Color it Green?**

Martha Johnson